4 pages 16 bars

a visual mixtape

SEQUENTIAL GRAFFITI

compiled and designed by
JIBA MOLEI ANDERSON

BLAXIS

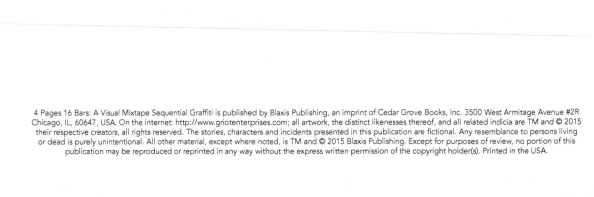

step into a world...

What you hold in your hands is a taste of what's to come...

4 Pages | 16 Bars: A Visual Mixtape began in 2013 as an art installation that ran for four months at Chicago institution **The Silver Room**. The event celebrated the cultural diversity of the independent comic book scene… And, was a stone groove, baby.

In 2015, diversity has become the buzzword in the comic book industry with companies like **DC** and **Marvel** claiming to lead the charge, but merely scratching the surface of the complexity and intersection of race, culture and gender.

The 4 Pages l 16 Bars: A Visual Mixtape trade paperback series will be a celebration of where true diversity exists in this industry, a sampler for potential fans to enjoy our intellectual properties, a showcase for existing and upcoming talent as well as a source guide for those fans to purchase our books.

The first volume will drop in **June 2015** with subsequent volumes coming out in **Fall 2015**, **Winter 2016** and **Spring 2016**.

The scene is more diverse than **Image** or **Dark Horse**. This is visual Jazz, Rock, Funk, Hip Hop and electronic music. This is art for the people.

We hope that you will step into the cypher and become a part of **The Blaxis**, an imprint of **Cedar Grove Books**.

BLAXIS

THE VISUAL MCs

kenjji jumanne-marshall
john jennings
n. steven harris
stacey robinson
micheline hess
jiba molei anderson
mark c. dudley
quinn mcgowan
ashley a. woods
jason reeves
stanley weaver
shawn alleyne
showari harrington
koi turnbull
philip johnson

4 pages 16 bars
a visual mixtape

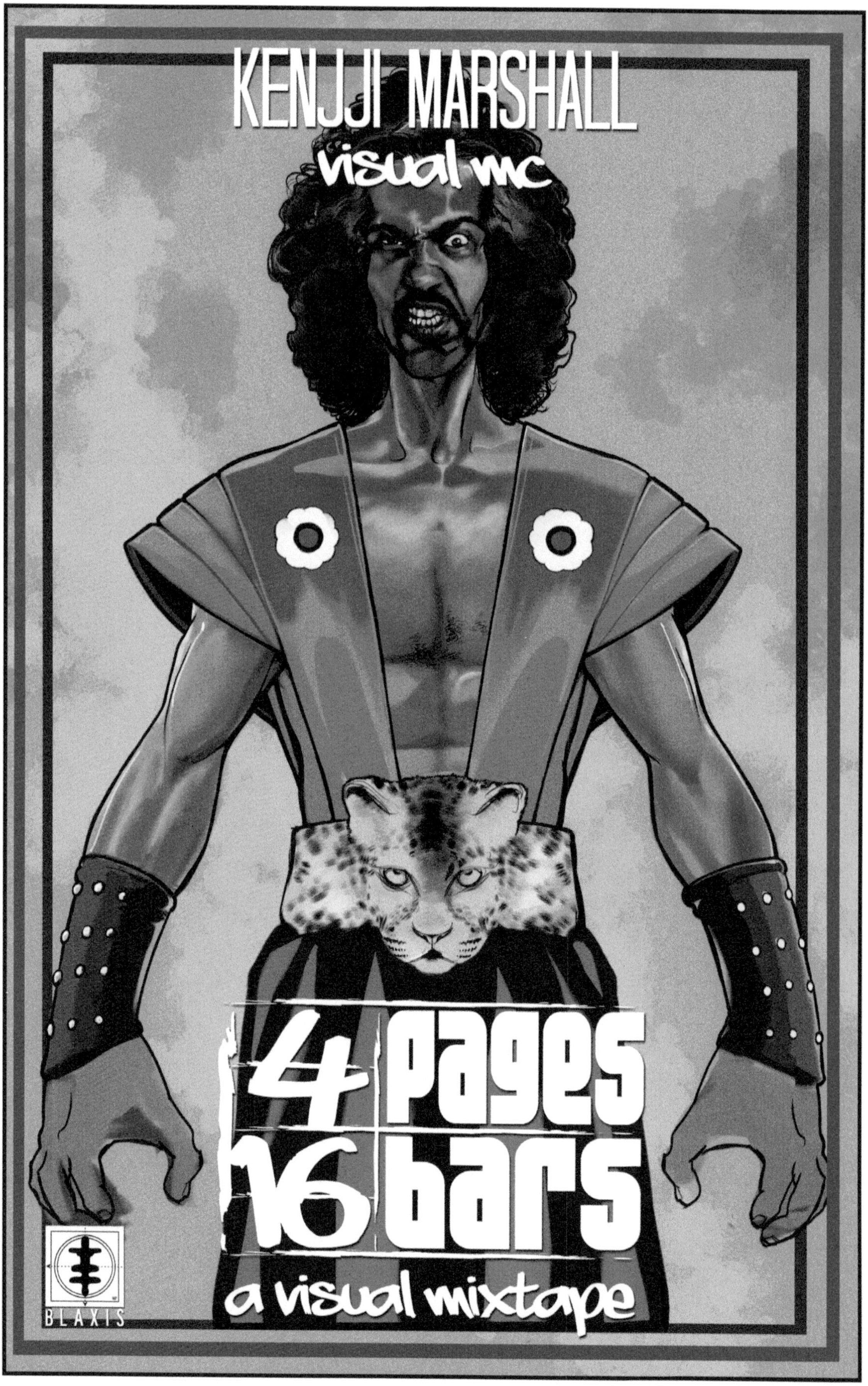
KENJJI MARSHALL
visual mc
4 pages
16 bars
a visual mixtape
BLAXIS

Kenjji Jumanne-Marshall is a freelance illustrator and comic artist whose work has appeared worldwide. A Detroit native, Kenjji includes 80's television, Hip Hop and the Motor City among his influences. Kenjji continues to work on new episodes of his true Voodoo action series *WitchDoctor* for **Griot Enterprises** and has recently published children's books like *Money Smart Kids* and *Read Roared the Lion* as well as producing artwork for MTV's *Teen Wolf*.

website: kenjji.com

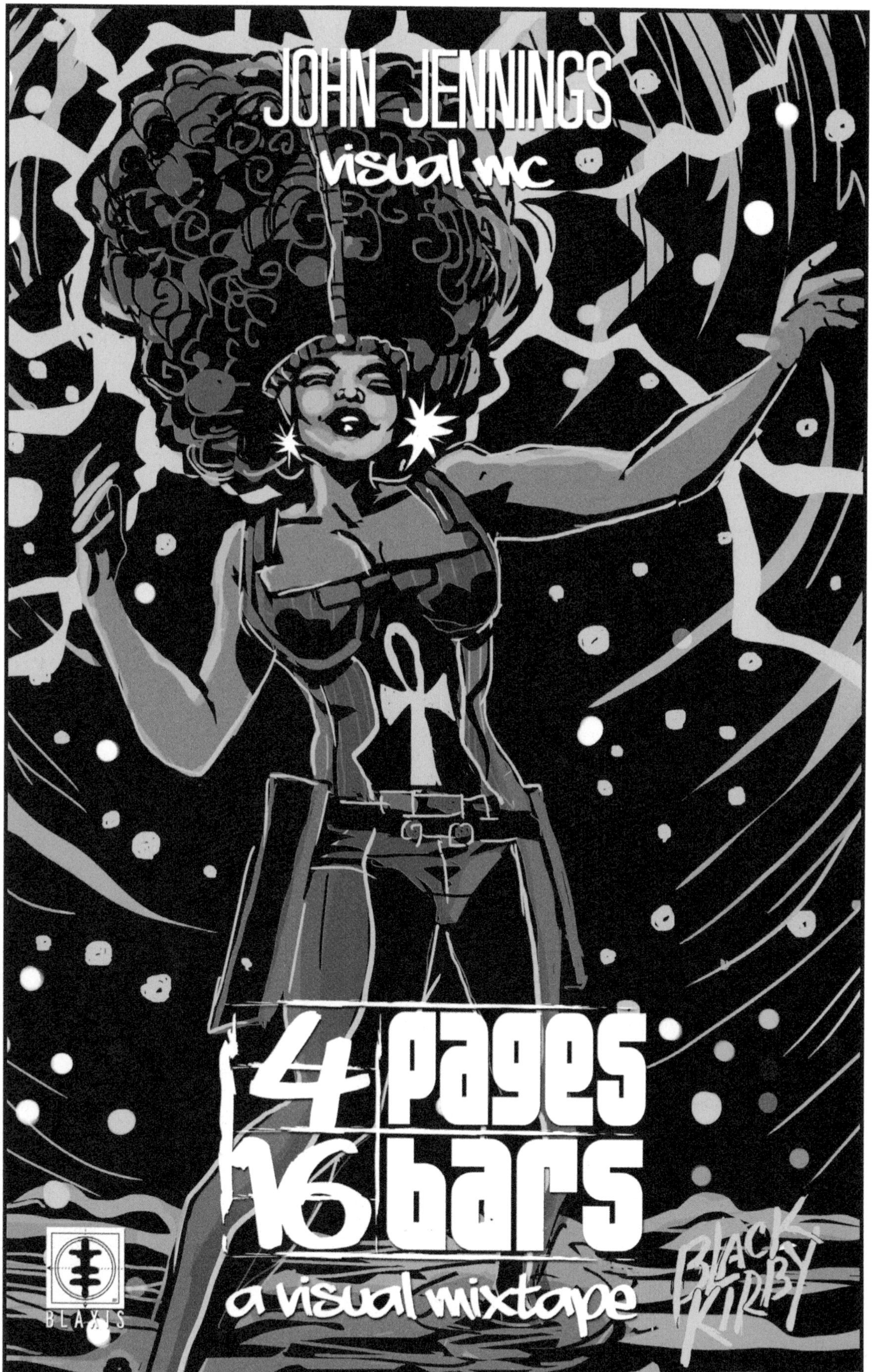
JOHN JENNINGS
visual mc
4 pages
16 bars
a visual mixtape
BLAXIS
BLACK KIRBY

John Jennings is an Associate Professor of Visual Studies at the **University of Buffalo SUNY**. His research and teaching focus on the analysis, explication, and disruption of African American stereotypes in popular visual media. He is an accomplished designer, curator, illustrator, and cartoonist.

Along with his long-time collaborator Damian Duffy, Jennings has co-authored and designed the books **Out of Sequence: Underrepresented Voices in American Comics, Black Comix: African American Independent Comics Art + Culture**, and the GLYPH Award winning graphic novel; **The Hole: Consumer Culture Vol. 1.**

His new projects include the supernatural crime story **Blue Hand Mojo: A Case of You** and the forthcoming graphic novel adaptation of Octavia Butler's classic dark fantasy novel **Kindred** (also with Duffy). He has also garnered acclaim for his artist collective **Black Kirby** along with his co-creator Stacey Robinson.

Currently, Jennings is working on among other things, **Kid Code: Channel Zero** with Stacey Robinson and Damian Duffy.

website: jjjennin70.tumblr.com

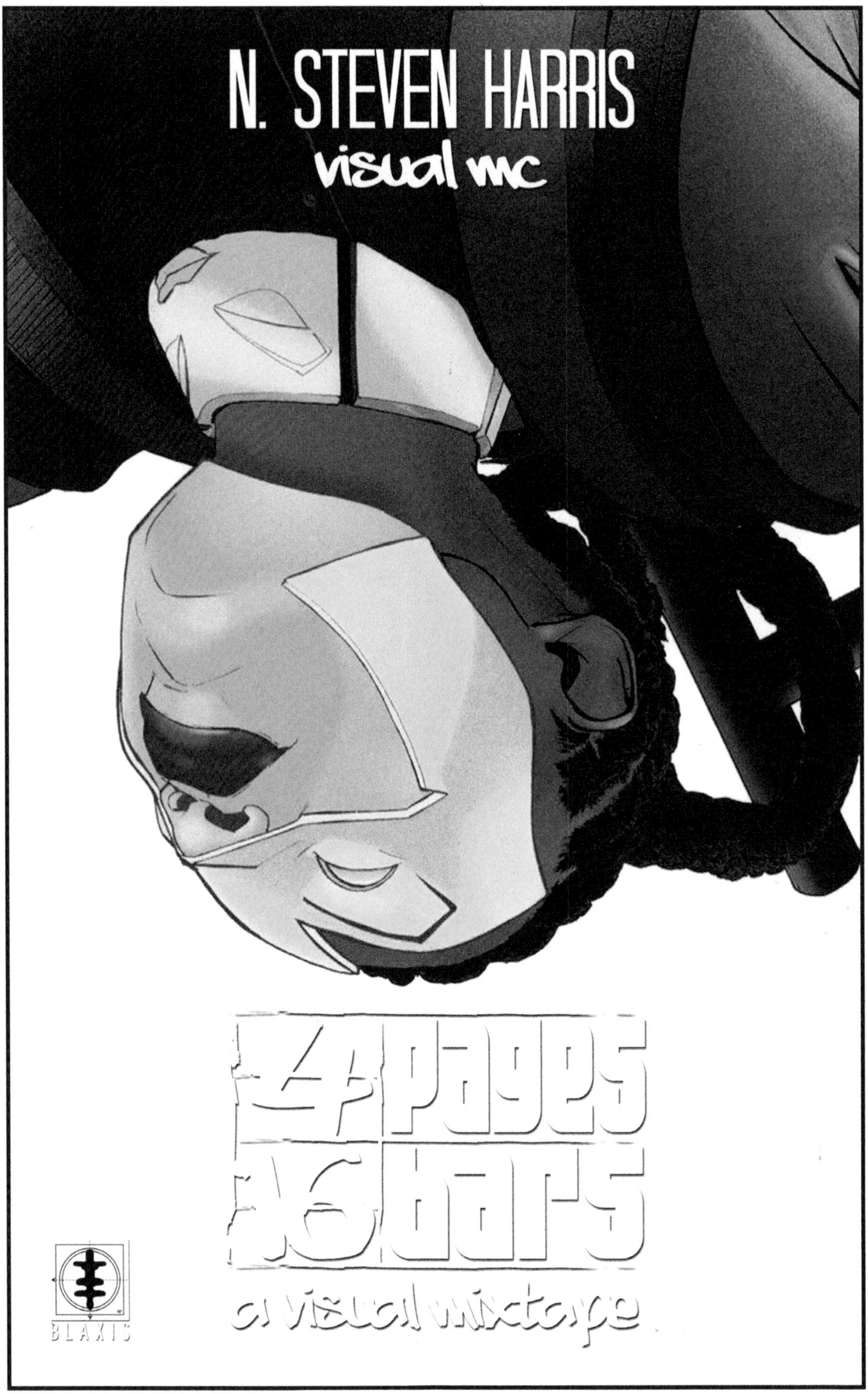
N. STEVEN HARRIS
visual mc
24 pages
16 bars
a visual mixtape
BLAXIS

N. Steven Harris is a professional comic book artist. He began his career in 1993 working for **Dark Horse Comics** on the title *Dark Horse Comics*. His first work for **DC Comics** was in 1993 in the title *Showcase '93*. He is also well known for his work on *Aztek: The Ultimate Man*.

N. Steven Harris has also created cover illustrations for **Warren Publications** in the 1990s. He has worked for Dark Horse Comics, making the *X* feature with writer Jerry Prosser. Harris other credits include *Robin* and *Black Lightning* at DC, as well as **Marvel's** *Cable*, *X Force* and *Deadpool*. Harris also co-created titles like *Crimson Rose*.

From the Glyph Award winning *Watson and Holmes* series, to the Glyph Award winning **Ajala** series, this person is puts his pencil where his mouth is. His credits also *Voltron* for *Dynamite Entertainment* and is currently working on his graphic novel entitled, *Brotherhood of the Fringe*.

website: nstevenworks.com/2005

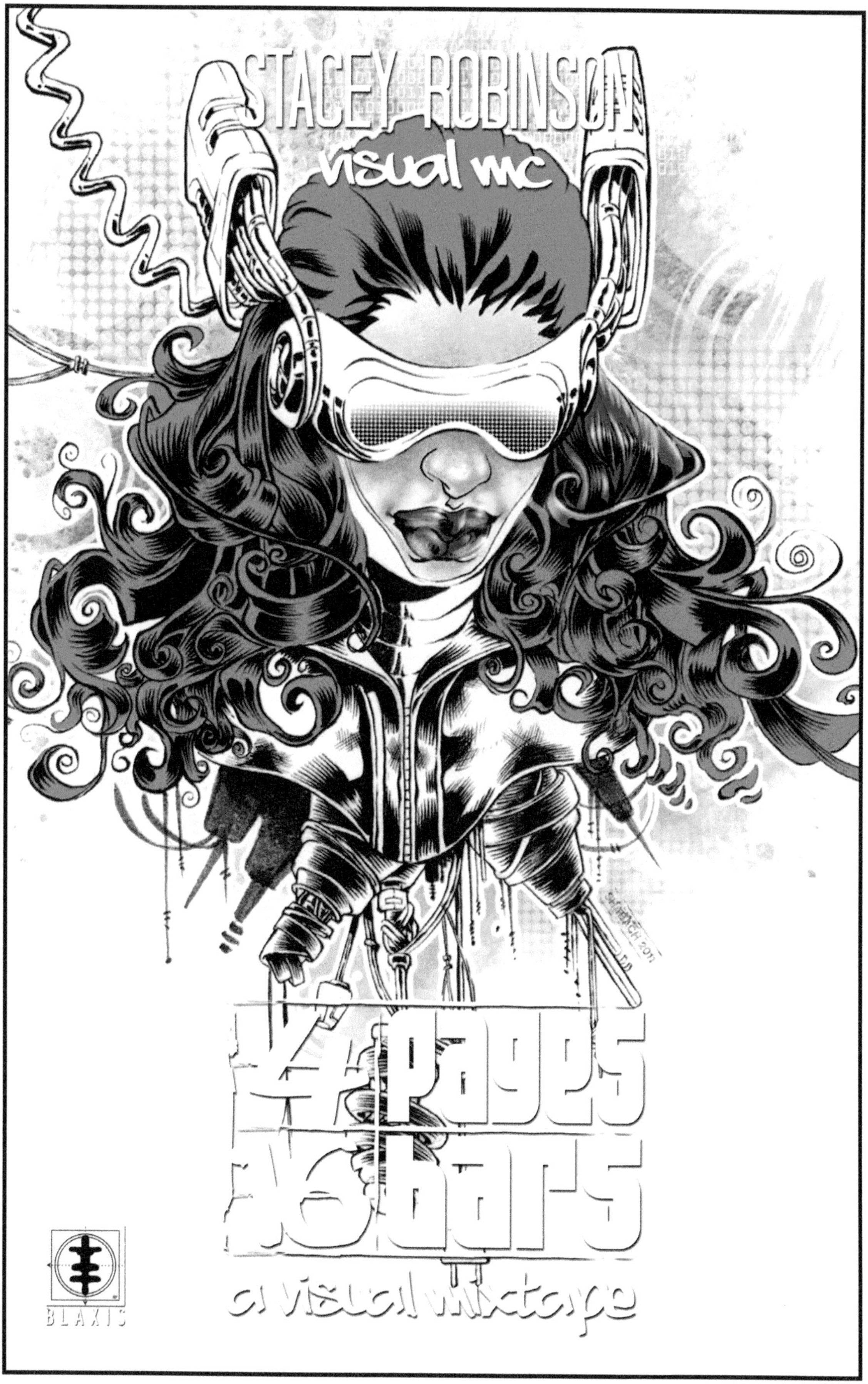
STACEY ROBINSON
visual mc
24 pages
16 bars
a visual mixtape
BLAXIS

Stacey Robinson is an artist. His subject matter examines the African-American experience, more specifically the future while making many African-American private conversations and concerns public.

In a celebratory fashion, he accentuates the form. What many times is over-sexualized is honored in his work as the accentuation, elongation and distortion of his forms represent much more than the initial appearance.

Inspired by Michelangelo, Ernie Barnes, Charles Bibbs and Robert Rauschenberg, Stacey ventured in a different direction, examining the future. His Afro-Futurist works consist of reoccurring motifs, which are symbols of technology and rebirth. Juxtaposing flesh with mechanical objects, the works comment on newness of life beyond the struggles of the past.

Stacey is the co-creator of **Rosarium Publishing's *Kid Code: Channel Zero***
with John Jennings and Damien Duffy.

website: staceyrobinson.tumblr.com

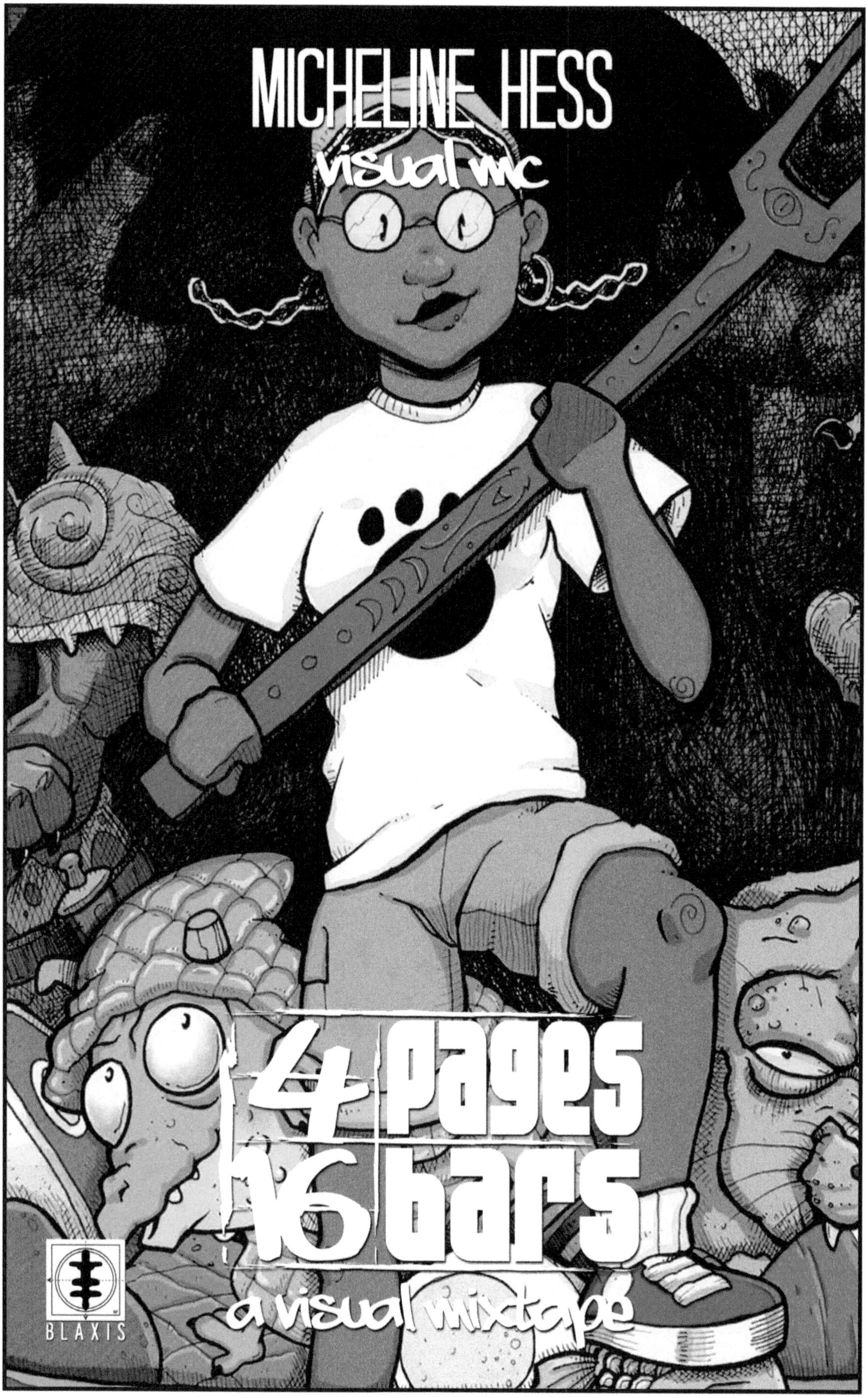
MICHELINE HESS
visual mc
4 pages
16 bars
a visual mixtape
BLAXIS

Born and raised in NYC, **Micheline Hess** does design at a prominent
ad agency in Chelsea and spends her spare time developing graphic novels,
short stories, and interactive iBooks for kids. She has always been fascinated
by the visual narrative in books and film and is constantly endeavoring to
weave her own sense of humorous story-telling into both her personal and
sometimes professional work.

Micheline is most adept at creating characters and stories that provide a safe
and fun way to inspire young children. Through colorful flights of fun and fancy,
she hopes to encourage a stronger sense of self-love, friendship, and a hunger
to embrace all things new and different in the world around them which is
evident in her creation for **Rosarium Publishing**, *Malice in Ovenland*.

website: about.me/kuronekko

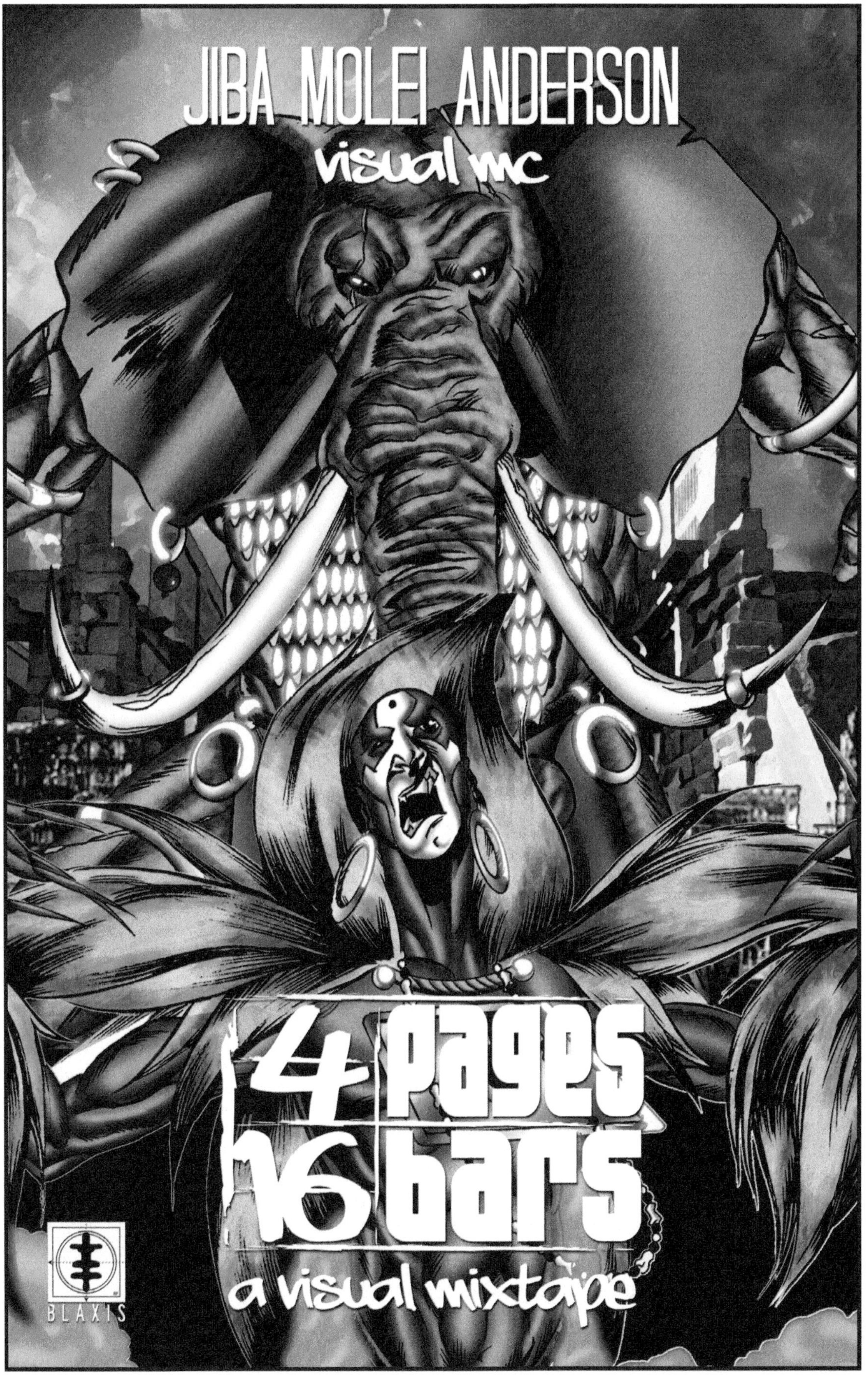
JIBA MOLEI ANDERSON
visual mc
4 pages
16 bars
a visual mixtape
BLAXIS

Jiba Molei Anderson is the owner of **Griot Enterprises** and creator of its flagship property *The Horsemen* and *Outworld: Return of the Master Teachers*. He has also written the educational text *Manifesto: The Tao of Jiba Molei Anderson*. Anderson is also Creative Director for **Cedar Grove Books** and maintains The Afrosoul Chronicles a blog dedicated to the discussion of race, politics and the business of popular culture.

Mr. Anderson is also a part of the fine art community having various one-man and group shows including being featured in the book *Black Comix* and guest lecturing at **The School of the Art Institute of Chicago** and *The* **Smithsonian National Museum of African Art** with The Horsemen's inclusion in The Smithsonian's permanent library.

In addition, Mr. Anderson has been interviewed for various publications such as **GQ Magazine, Afropunk, Sci Fi Pulse** and the **New York Times** and has written articles for various magazines such as LaRana de Sevilla and online journals.

Currently, Mr. Anderson is a Part-Time Lecturer at **Chicago State University**, teaching courses in Animation, Multimedia and Video Game Design and speaks across the country promoting comic books and graphic novels as tools for education in the exploration of race, culture and identity. He recently created ***The Song of Lionogo: An Indian Ocean Mythological Remix*** for the Smithsonian National Museum of African Art.

website: griotenterprises.com

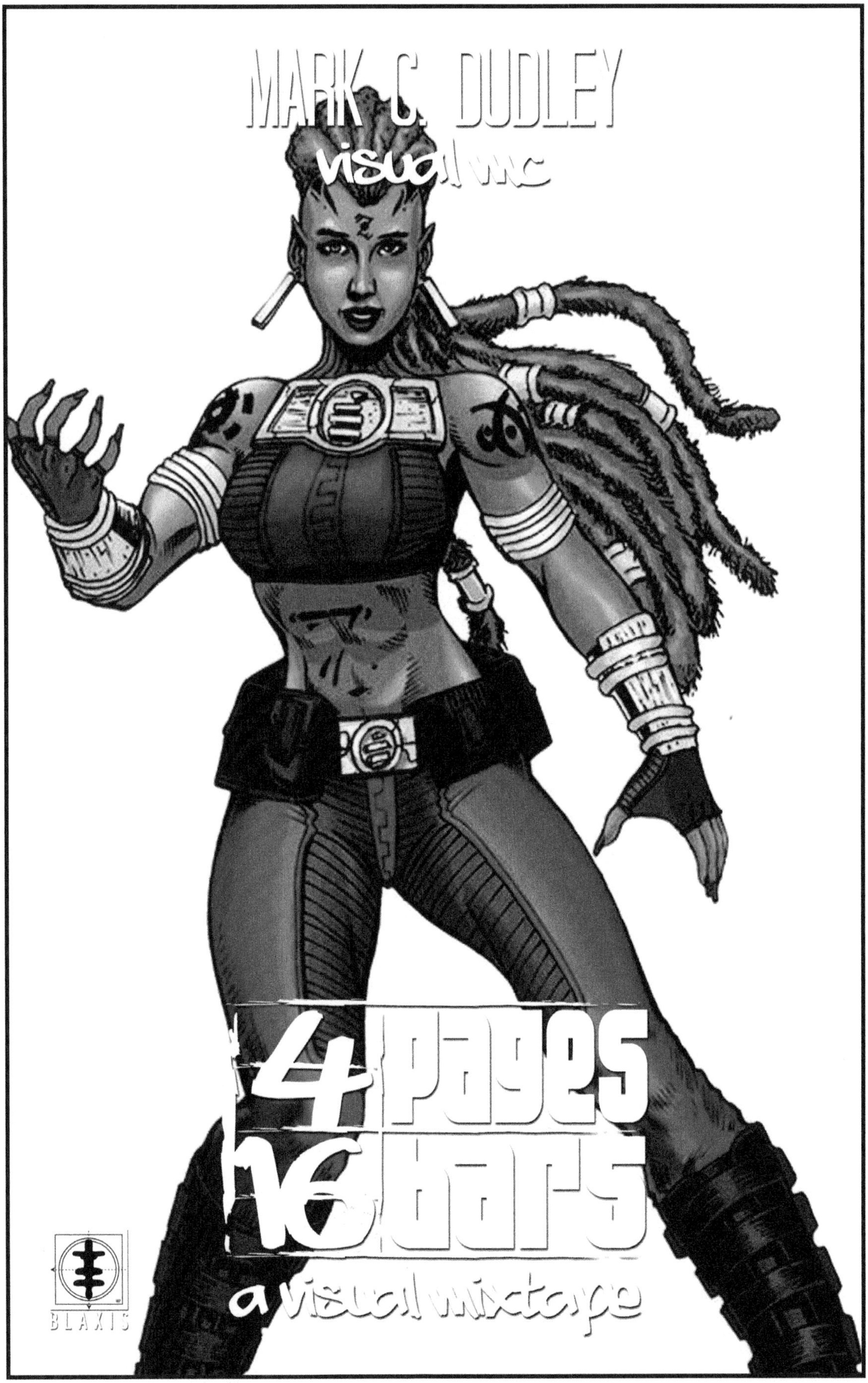
MARK C. DUDLEY
visual mc
4 pages
16 bars
a visual mixtape
BLAXIS

Mark C. Dudley is native of the Detroit Area. His love affair with artwork and comics started when he was a child, but his imagination found a new forum when he discovered the role-playing games of **Palladium Books**. Mark's first and all-time favorite *Palladium RPG: Heroes Unlimited™*. His next favorite: *Rifts®*.

His work appears under his own name as well as under **Drunken Style Studios** in many issues of The Rifter® as well as such notable RPG titles as *Heroes Unlimited™ RPG 2nd Edition, Armageddon Unlimited™, Rifts® Ultimate Edition, Rifts® New West™, Rifts® China Two, Rifts® MercTown™, Rifts® Merc Ops, Nightbane® Survival Guide, Heroes of the Megaverse®* and many others.

Mark Dudley's collaborations have gone beyond artwork on numerous Palladium projects, including concept and concept development, talent coordination, and work on one of Palladium's ill-fated MMORPG projects. Mark led a handpicked crew of artists and writers from Drunken Style Studios to develop a mature-themed Nightbane® animated TV series that Palladium hopes will someday find a home on a cable channel.

He is also the creator of the Afro futuristic ***Juda Fist: 7 Deaths of the Yobi***. This dystopian, hip hop inspired tale is about Amaru Jones, a man turned into a bio organic weapon who awakes from a decades old sleep to rebuild his life. However, age old enemies await his resurrection and ready themselves to continue a battle in which the fate of our solar system hangs in the balance.

website: markcdudley.deviantart.com/?mrd*35936

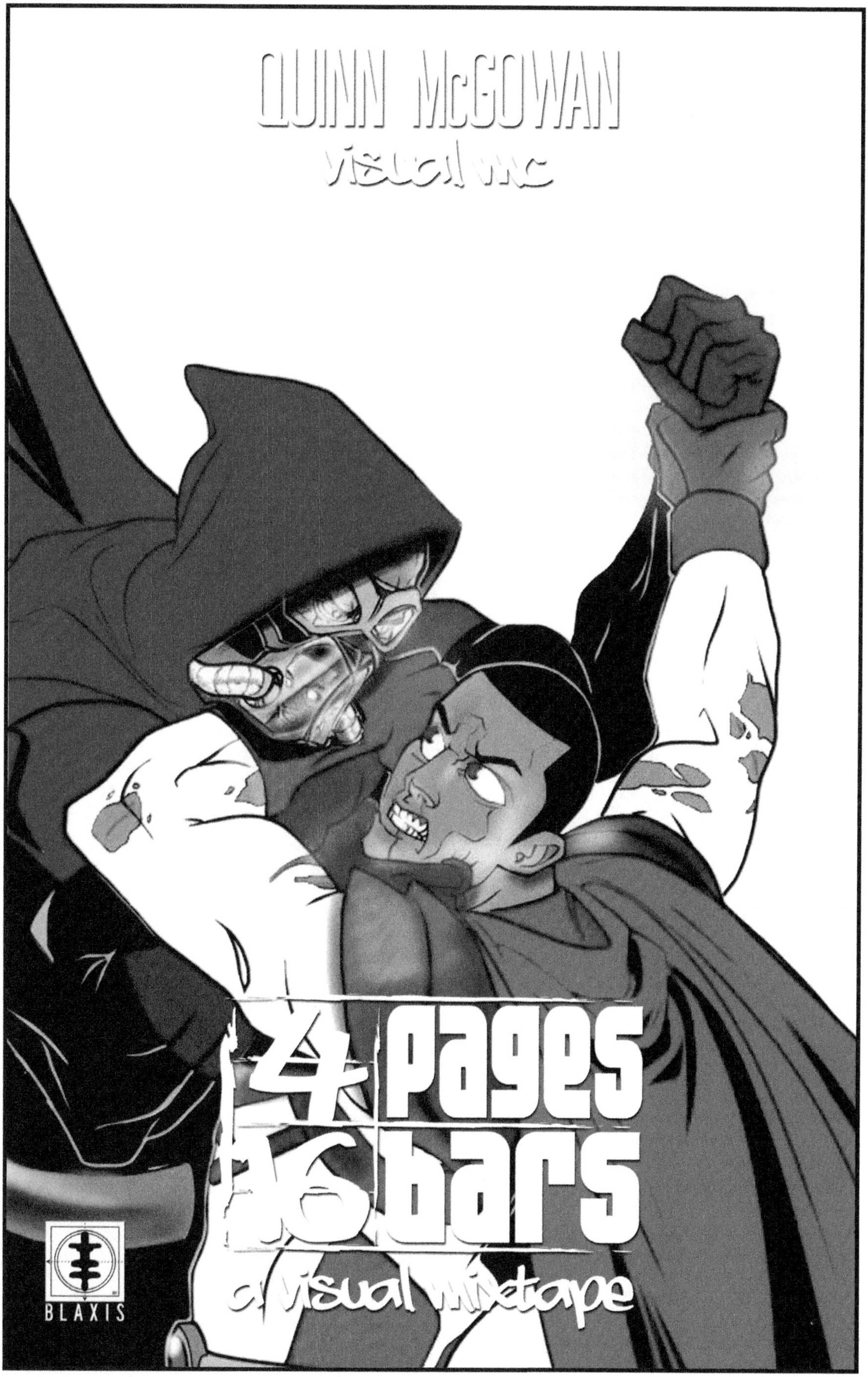
QUINN McGOWAN
visual mc
4 pages
16 bars
a visual mixtape
BLAXIS

Quinn McGowan (known to friends as "The Mighty Quinn," "TattQ" or "Quotable Quinn McGowan") is a comic book creator, licensed tattoo artist, visual artist and performer with the Memphis-based hip hop group the **Iron Mic Coalition** (IMC). His visual mediums include body art, digital art, paint and his first love, comic art.

He is the creator of **Project: WILDFIRE** and half of the duo responsible for the upcoming comic *Wild Kingdoms: WarBear vs. BattleBunny*.

Quinn lives in Memphis, TN with his wife and three children.

website: quinnproart.com

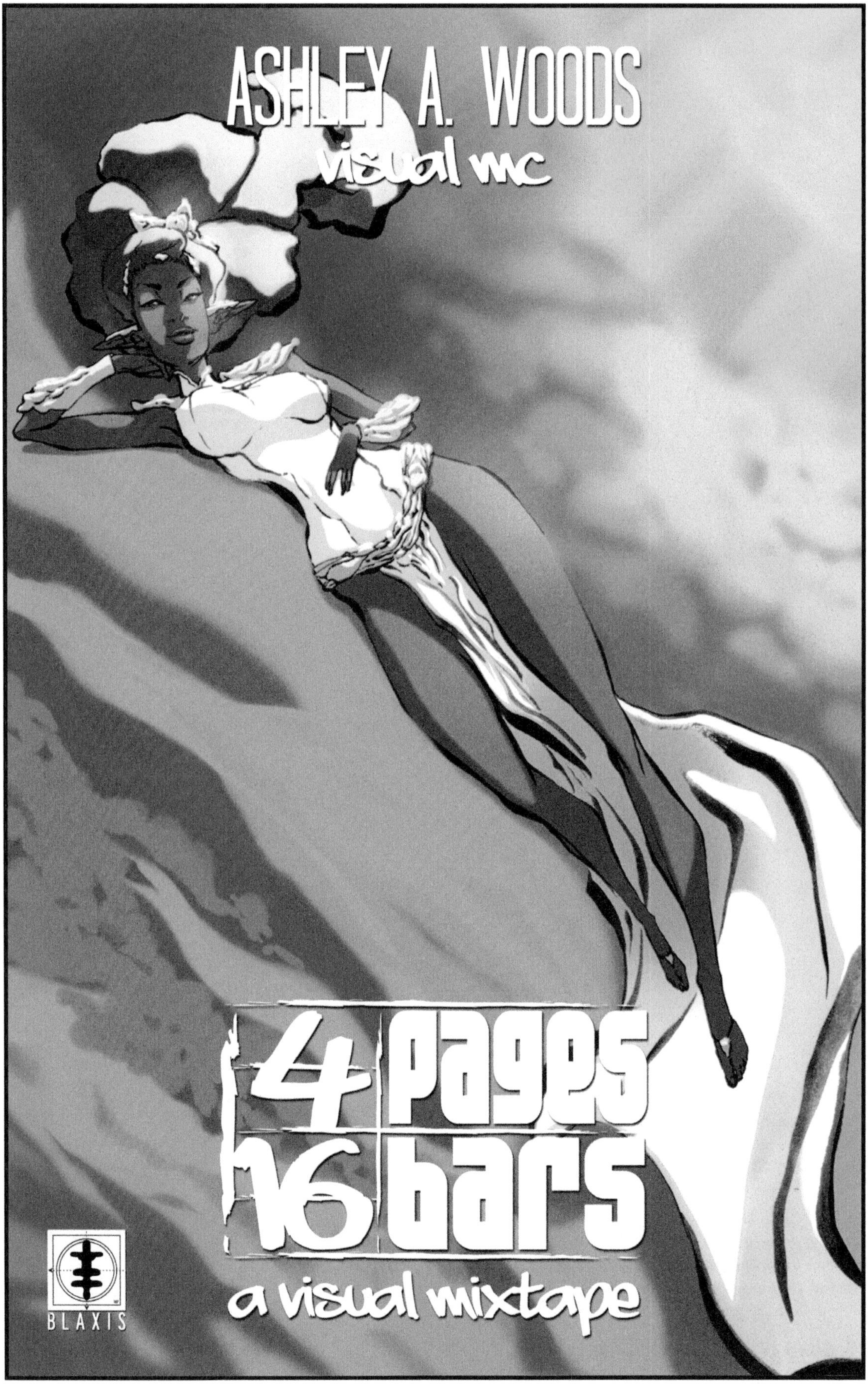

ASHLEY A. WOODS
visual mc
4 pages
16 bars
a visual mixtape
BLAXIS

Born and raised in Chicago, **Ashley A. Woods** is an illustrator who got her start through self-publishing her action-fantasy comic series, *Millennia War*, while attending the International Academy of Design and Technology.

After earning her degree in Video and Animation, she traveled to Kyoto, Japan, where she presented her work in a gallery showcase called *Out Of Sequence*. Her work has also been included in *Black Comix: African American Independent Comics, Art and Culture* (edited by Damian Duffy and John Jennings). When Ashley isn't working, she enjoys playing video games and studying Japanese.

website: ashleyawoods.com

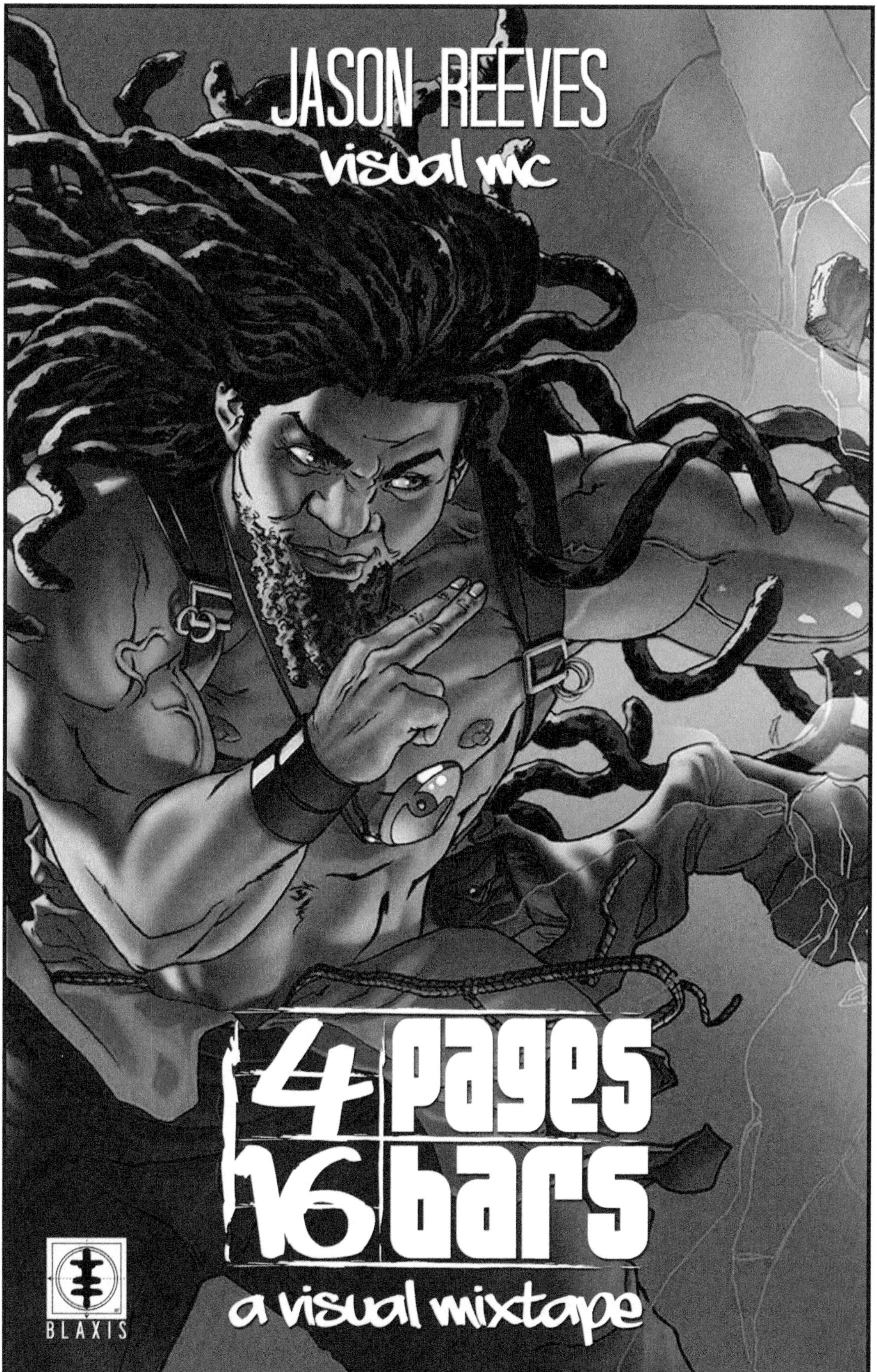
JASON REEVES
visual mc
4 pages
16 bars
a visual mixtape
BLAXIS

Jason Reeves is a Los Angeles-based comics creator who has had his comics work published by **USA Today**, **Devil's Due Publishing** and **Arcana Studios**. In addition to comics, he has done illustration for Esquire Magazine, USAToday. com's 'F-00 Fighters' series and HASBRO's G.I. Joe and Transformers toylines. He is currently working on the award-winning *OneNation* comic series with Alverne Ball and is co-owner of the design studio **133Art**.

website: 133art.com

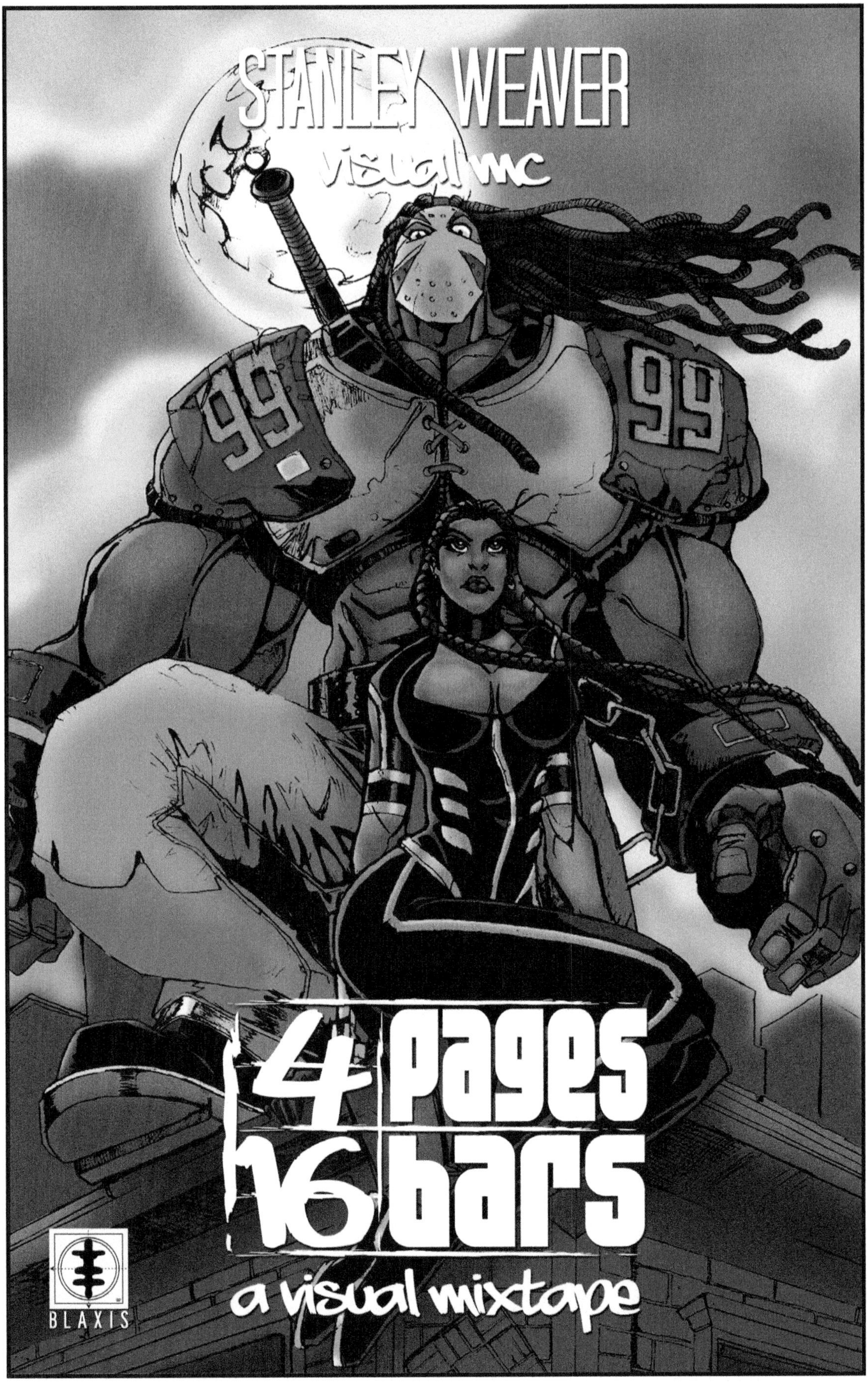
STANLEY WEAVER
visual mc
99
99
4 pages
16 bars
a visual mixtape
BLAXIS

Stanley "Standingo" Weaver is a man of contradictions. He's a big man who loves to laugh and has a quick wit, yet he is serious about his artwork. He has produced covers for Milton Davis' **NV Media** and interiors Aminah Armour's *Dziva Jones*. Stanley is co-creator of the ***Almighty Street Team*** with Joe Robinson Currie, Shawn Alleyne and James Mason.

website: standingo73.deviantart.com

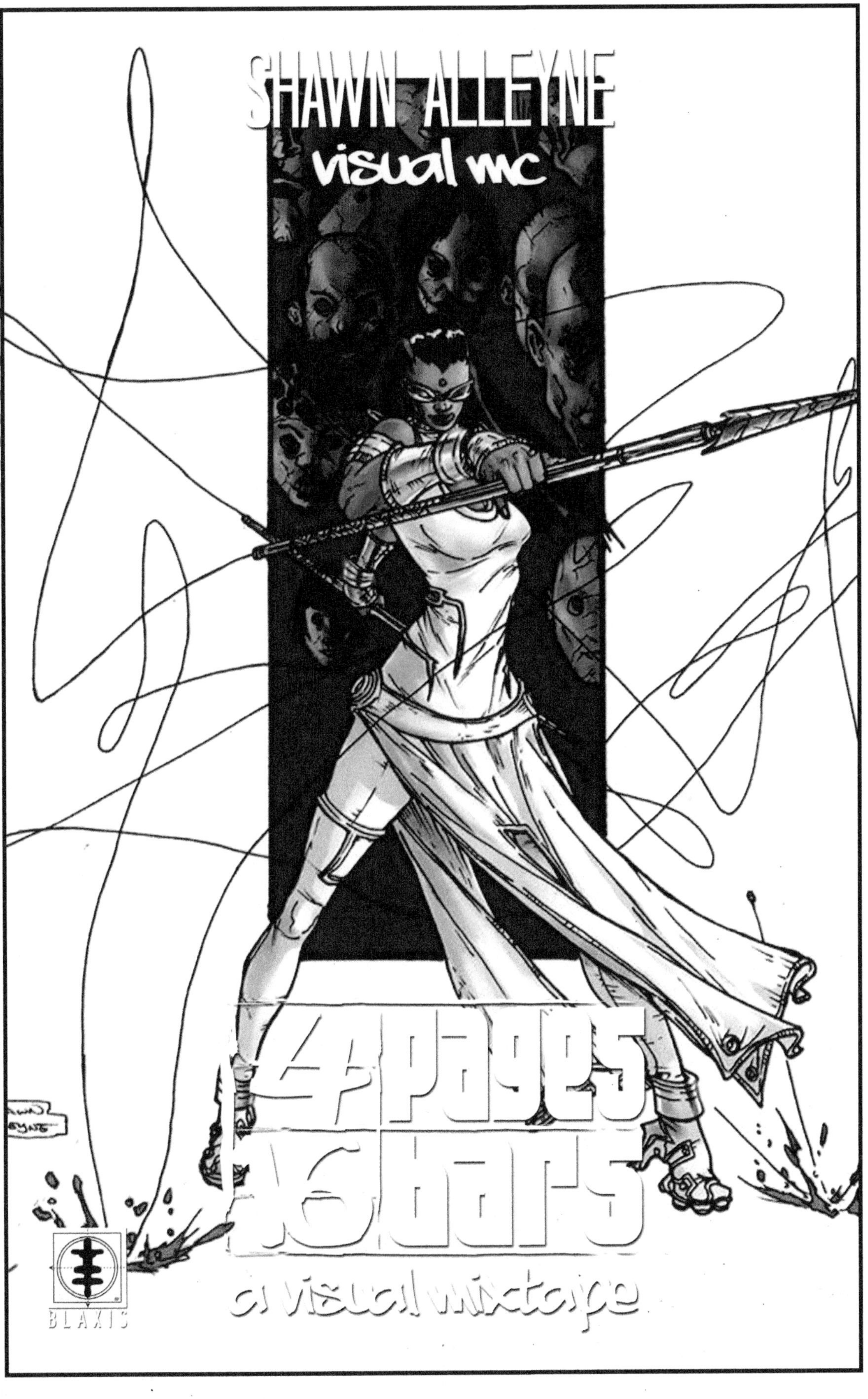
SHAWN ALLEYNE
visual mc
4 pages
16 bars
a visual mixtape
BLAXIS

Shawn Alleyne was born and raised on the island of Barbados, but later relocated to Philadelphia in his teens, and has lived there since. From an early age he knew he wanted to be involved in art in some capacity, and is currently working in the demanding field of freelance art as a writer, inker and instructor.

He is also the founder of the art group **Artmada** and the networking group **Xion**, with branches in Philly, New York and more. Shawn's work is produced under the **Pyroglyphics Studios** banner, a name roughly translated to mean "Hot Images," to reflect his gritty self-taught style.

Currently, Shawn is co-creator of ***The Almighty Street Team*** with Joe Robinson Currie, Stanley Weaver and James Mason.

website: pyroglyphics1.deviantart.com

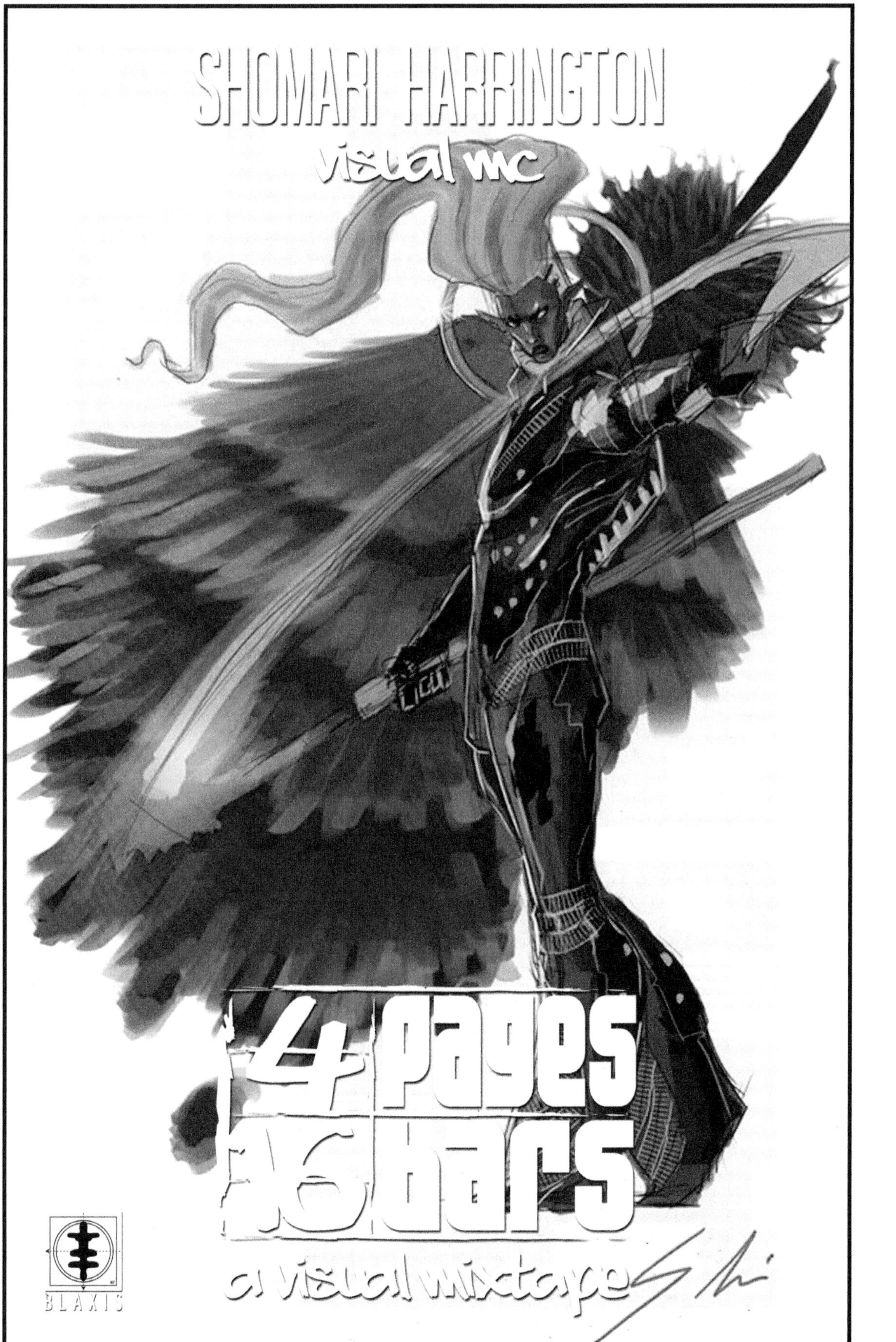
SHOMARI HARRINGTON
visual mc
4 pages 16 bars
a visual mixtape
BLAXIS

Shomari Harrington is a Visual Artist born and raised in Chicago. From an early age, he has always been fascinated by the wonders of what a pencil and a sheet of paper could create. The desire and passion to create has helped him to become the artist that he is today.

Shomari graduated with a Bachelor degree in Film majoring in Animation from **Columbia College Chicago**, where he learned from some of the best and brightest in the field of Film & Animation. Shomari has also worked closely with professional comic book artist as an intern at **Four Star Studios**, located in Chicago, Illinois.

In early 2014, his desire to become a better artist lead him to study abroad at Tongji University in Shanghai, China. Upon his return to the U.S., Shomari has vigorously pursued numerous projects, film/animation and illustration, with release dates in 2015. Shomari's Art work has also appeared at the *Milestones: African American in Comics, Pop Culture and Beyond* gallery hosted at the **Geppi Museum of Entertainment** in Baltimore, MD.

Shomari is an artist who enjoys working with others on a team, being productive, and creating thought provoking works of art. Currently Shomari works as an Illustrator/Animator at **Hi5 Design Studio** in Chicago, IL.

website: shomariharrington.com

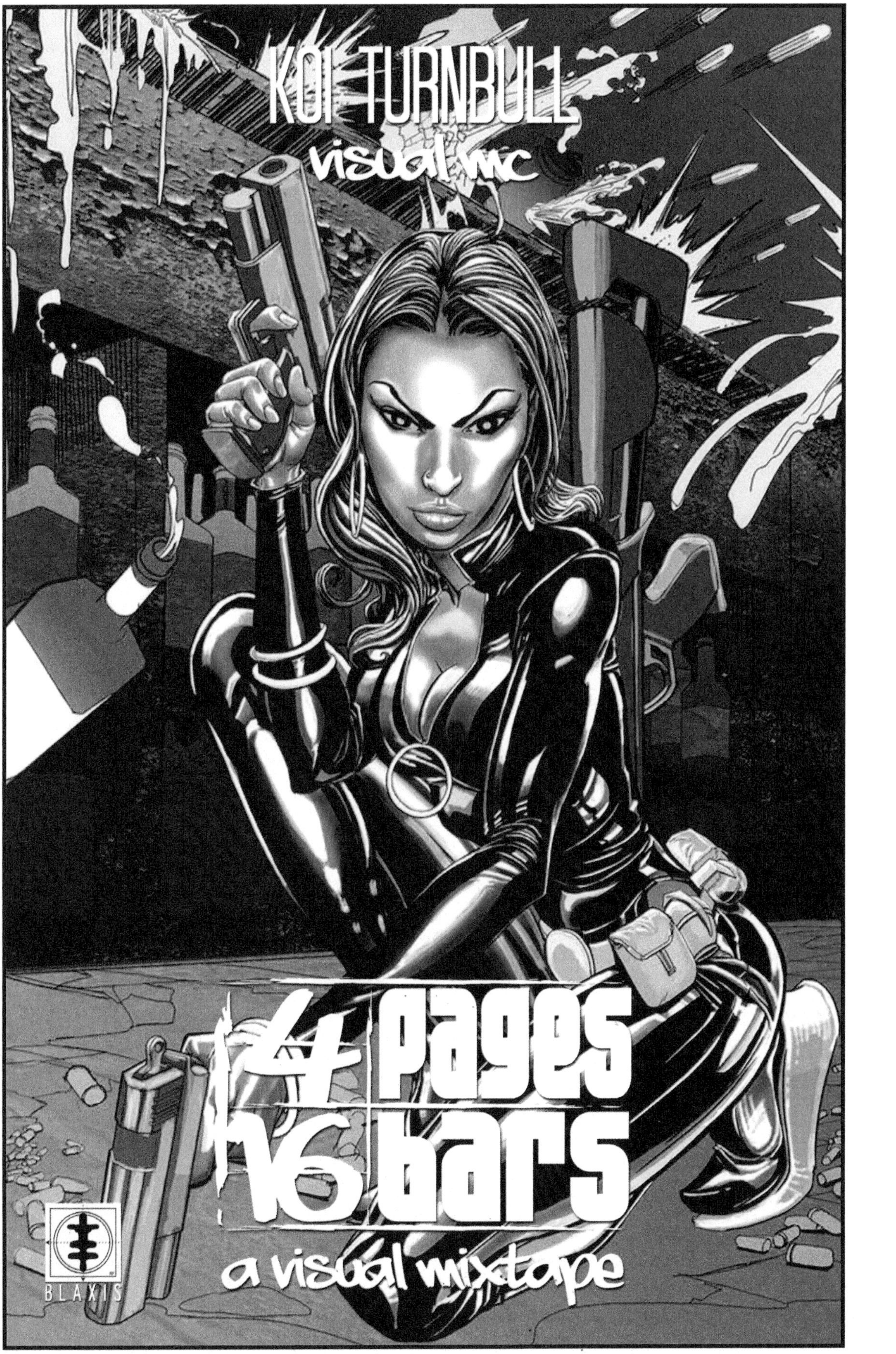
KOI TURNBULL
visual mc
4 pages
16 bars
a visual mixtape
BLAXIS

Koi Turnbull was born December 12, 1976 in Elmhurst, Queens NY. He began work as a background artist on Marvel projects for Adam Pollian and Walter McDaniel.

Koi's big break happened during the 2002 Wizard World Chicago Comic Convention, at a portfolio review with Aspen MLT's Frank Mastromauro (Executive Vice President) and Peter Steigerwald (Vice President of Publishing) of **Aspen MLT**.

After receiving the penciler job with Aspen MLT, Koi moved to S anta Monica, CA to work in the Marina Del Rey studio. Working under the direction of Michael Turner, Koi's talent grew, and with that followed Mike's run on **Fathom** with his own run starting with Fathom Volume 2. Not feeling hindered by the large fan following of Mike's work, Koi was able to follow Mike's work with his own and bring his influence to the comic during his run.

Following Koi's run on Fathom, Koi has worked with **DC Comics** including *Flash*, and *Superman Confidential*, **Marvel Comics** including *Terror INC*, *New Warriors*, *Black Panther* and the *One Month 2 Live* storyline as well as other comic projects.

website: cartoonrealism.wix.com/koiturnbull

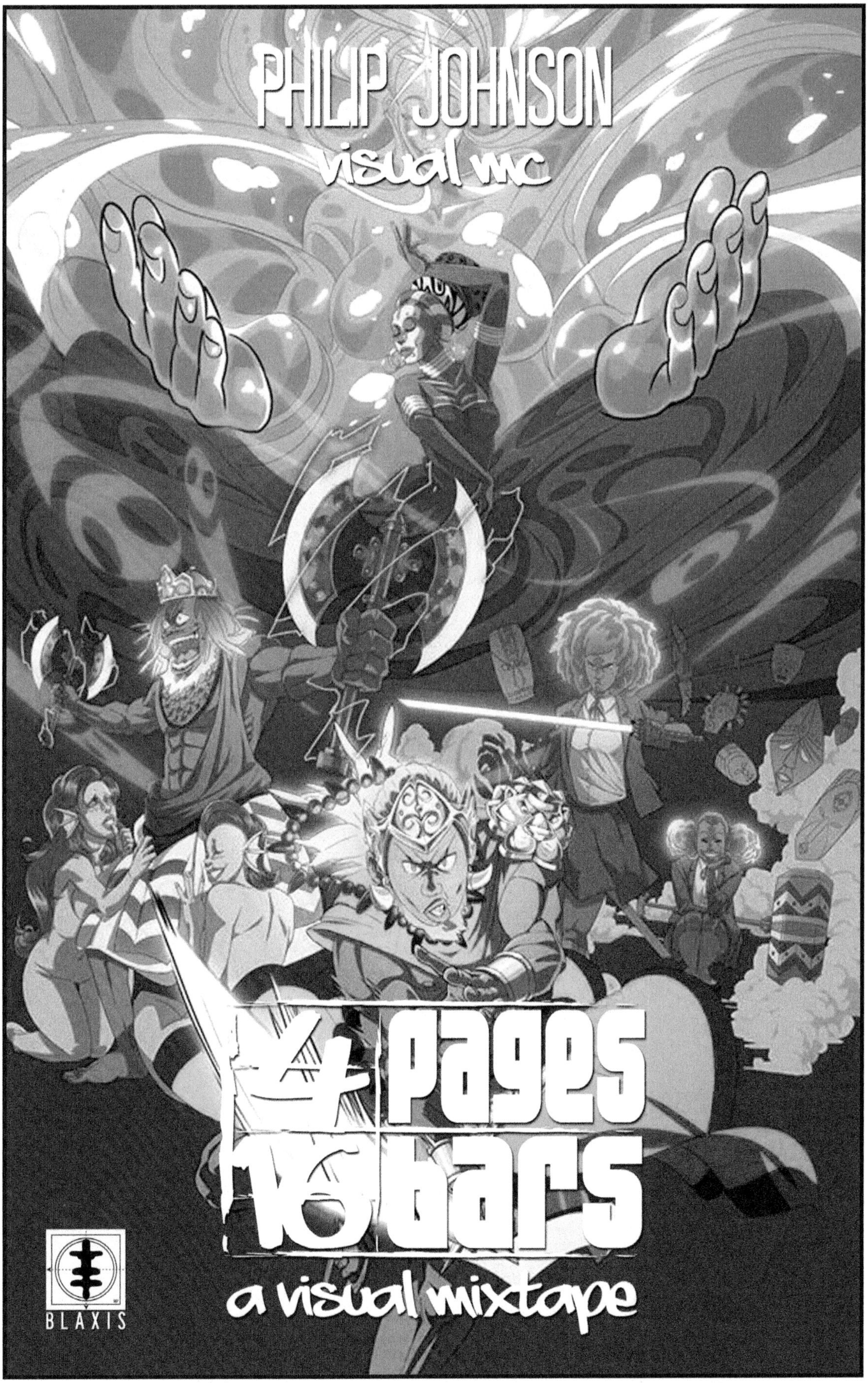
PHILIP JOHNSON
visual mc
4 pages
16 bars
a visual mixtape
BLAXIS

Philip Johnson is a freelance artist and animator living in Richmond, Virginia. He is an extremely talented individual just tryin' to live life on his own terms. He loves cartoons and comic books.

His favorite food is pizza, his favorite video games are fighting games, and he'll listen to any kind of music. Philip wishes he had more to say, but he doesn't think he's really that interesting...

website: signsoflifeonmars.deviantart.com/?rurd*24089

THE LITERARY DJs

bill campbell
ytasha l. womack
milton davis
roosevelt pitt
andre batts
la morris richmond
todd johnson
aminah amour
geoffrey thorne
brandon easton
brandon thomas
jude w. mire
joe robinson currie
damion gonzales

a visual mixtape

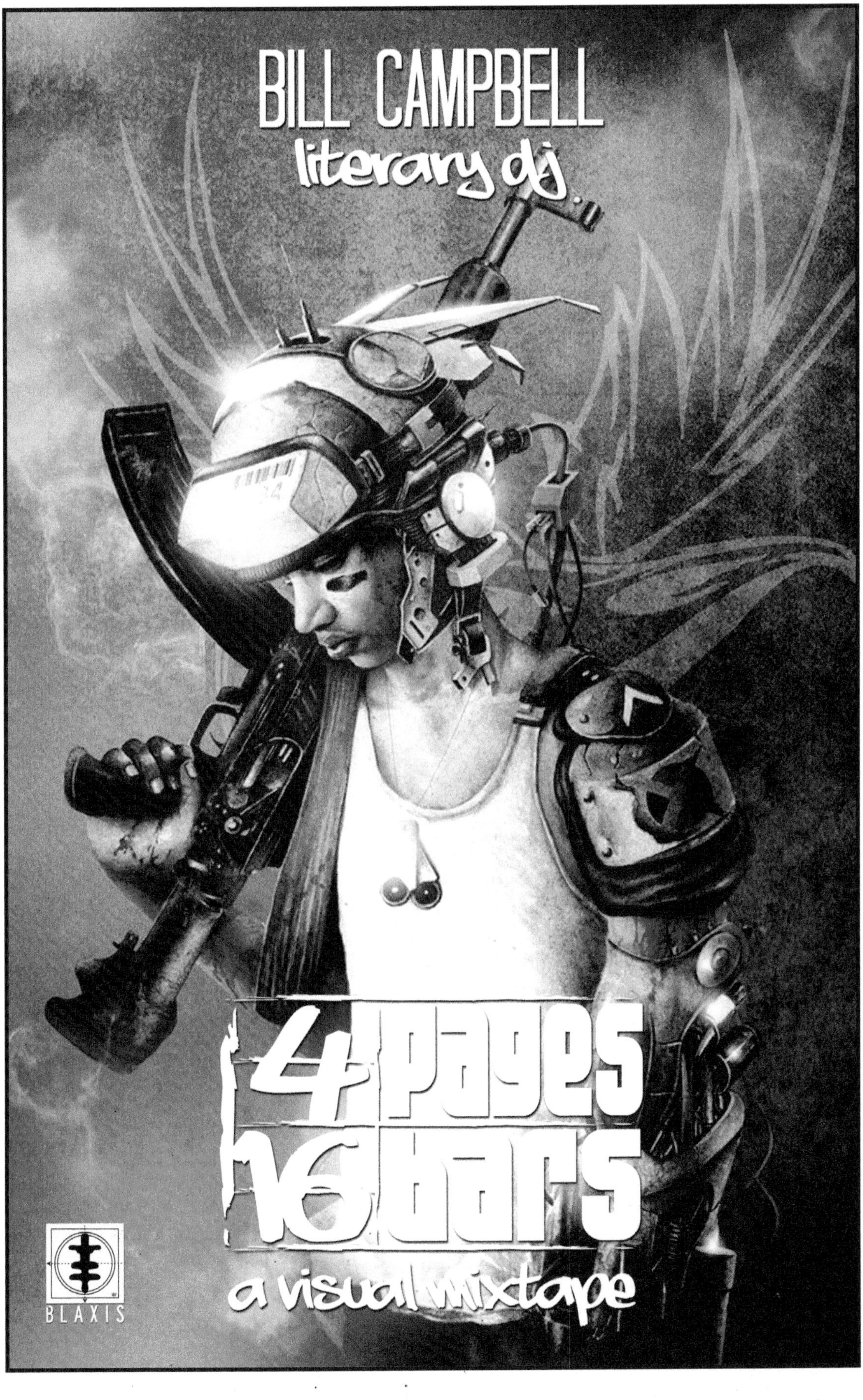
BILL CAMPBELL
literary dj
4 pages
16 bars
a visual mixtape
BLAXIS

Bill Campbell is the author of **Sunshine Patriots**, *My Booty Novel*, and *Pop Culture: Politics, Puns, "Poohbutt" from a Liberal Stay-at-Home Dad and Koontown Killing Kaper*. Along with Edward Austin Hall, he co-edited the groundbreaking anthology, *Mothership: Tales from Afrofuturism and Beyond*. Campbell lives in Washington, DC, where he spends his time with his family, helps produce audio books for the blind, and helms **Rosarium Publishing**.

website: rosariumpublishing.com

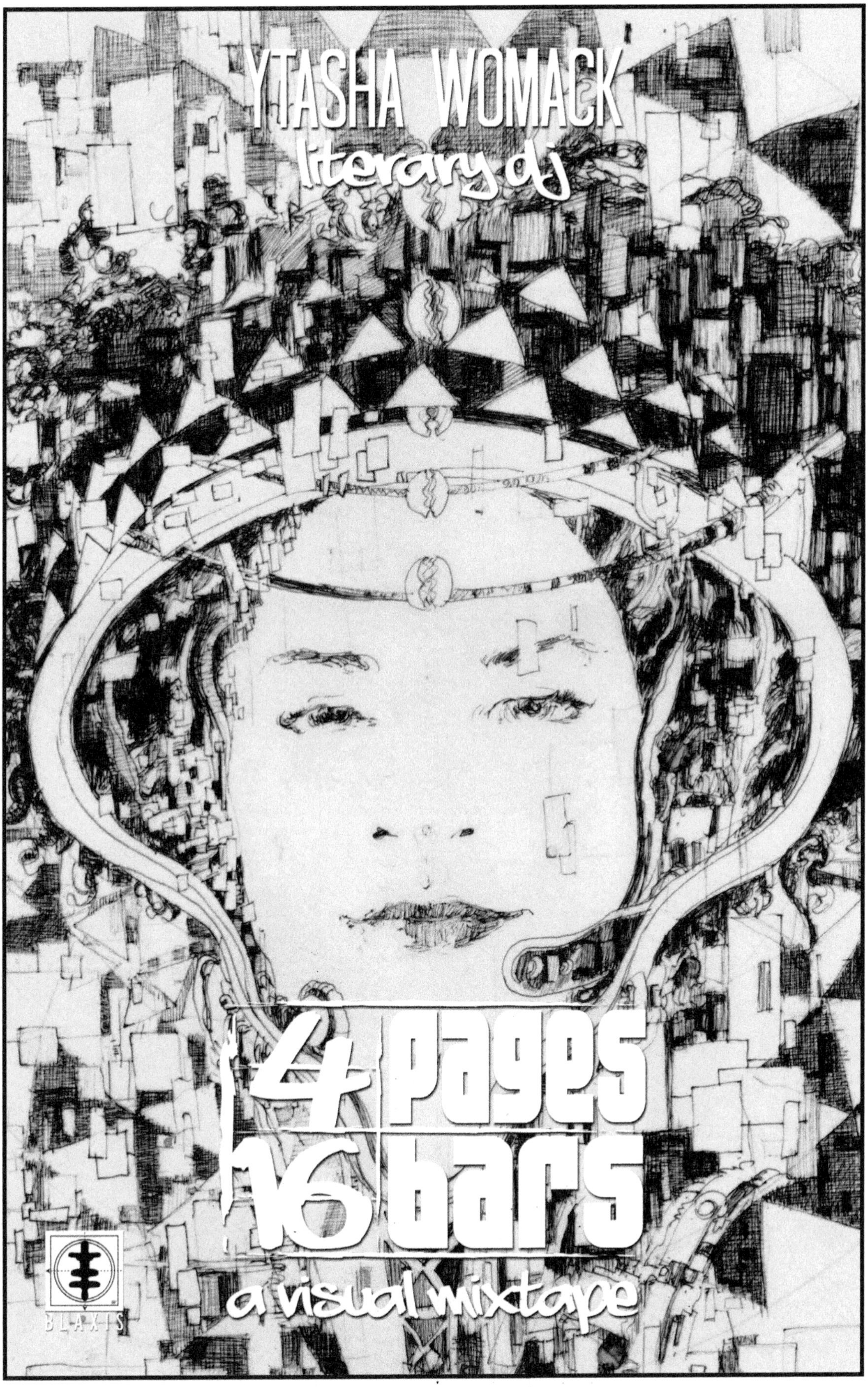
YTASHA WOMACK
literary dj
4 pages
16 bars
a visual mixtape
BLAXIS

Ytasha L. Womack is an award-winning filmmaker/author/journalist and choreographer. She is author/creator of the popfuturist/afrofuturist novel *2212:Book of Rayla*, first of the groundbreaking Rayla 2212 series. Her other books include the critically acclaimed book *Post Black: How a New Generation is Redefining African American Identity* (Lawrence Hill Books). Post Black was hailed as a Booklists' Top Black History Reader of 2010 and is a popular cultural studies text universities across the US.

She also co-edited the anthology *Beats, Rhymes and Life: What We Love and Hate About Hip Hop* (Harlem Moon/Random House). A Chicago native, her film projects include *The Engagement* (director) and *Love Shorts* (producer/writer). Ytasha is currently editor of the cultural news site www.postblackexperience.com and a guest editor for **NV Magazine**.

A social media and pop culture expert, she frequently consults and guest lectures for corporations and universities across the world.

website: rayla2212.com

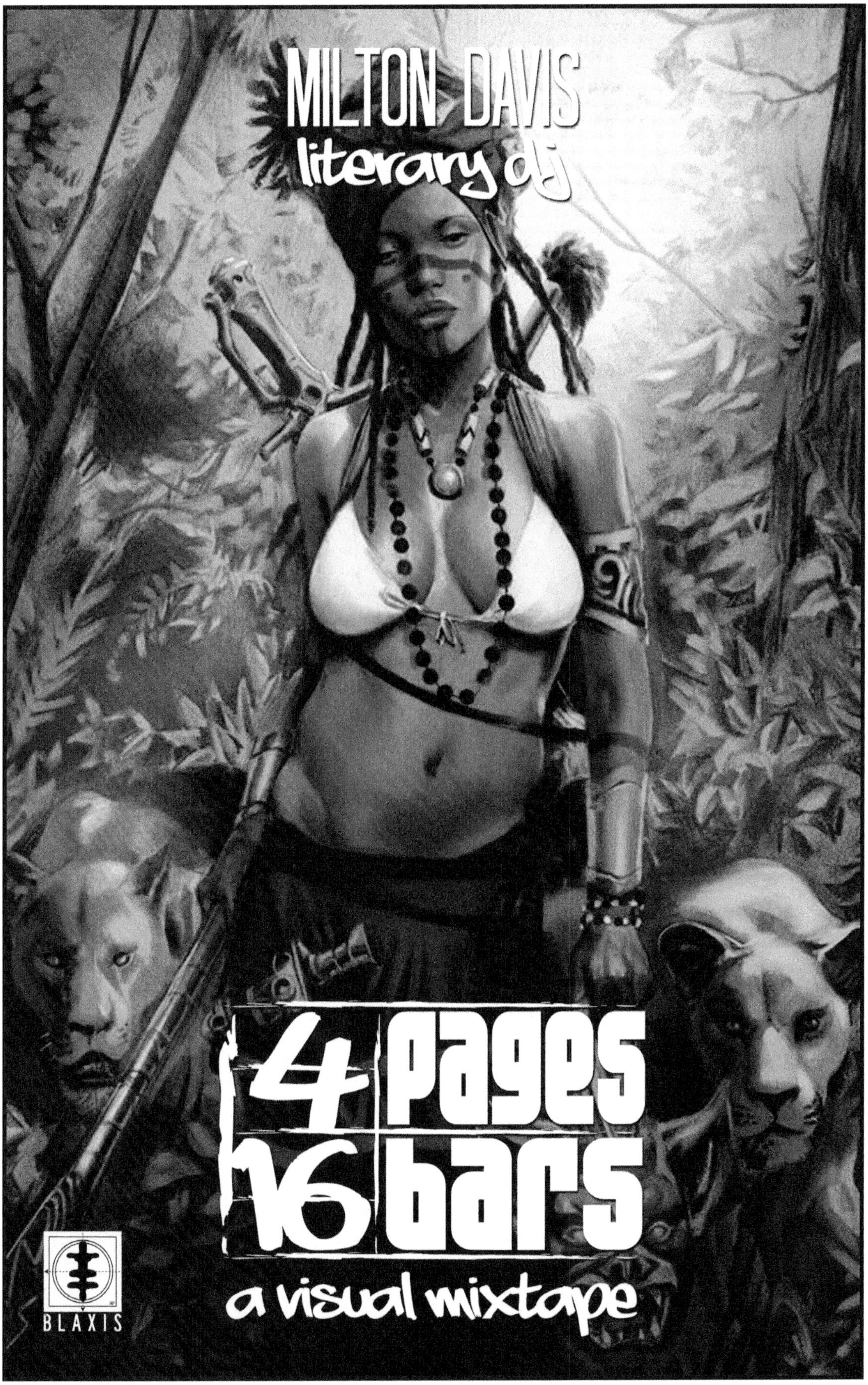
MILTON DAVIS
literary dj
4 pages
16 bars
a visual mixtape
BLAXIS

Milton Davis is owner of **MVmedia, LLC** , a micro publishing company specializing in Science Fiction, Fantasy and Sword and Soul. MVmedia's mission is to provide speculative fiction books that represent people of color in a positive manner.

Milton is the author of eight novels; his most recent **The Woman of the Woods** and *Amber and the Hidden City*. He is co-editor of four anthologies; *Griots: A Sword and Soul Anthology* and *Griot: Sisters of the Spear*, with Charles R. Saunders; *The Ki Khanga Anthology* with Balogun Ojetade and the *Steamfunk! Anthology*, also with Balogun Ojetade.

website: mvmediaatl.com

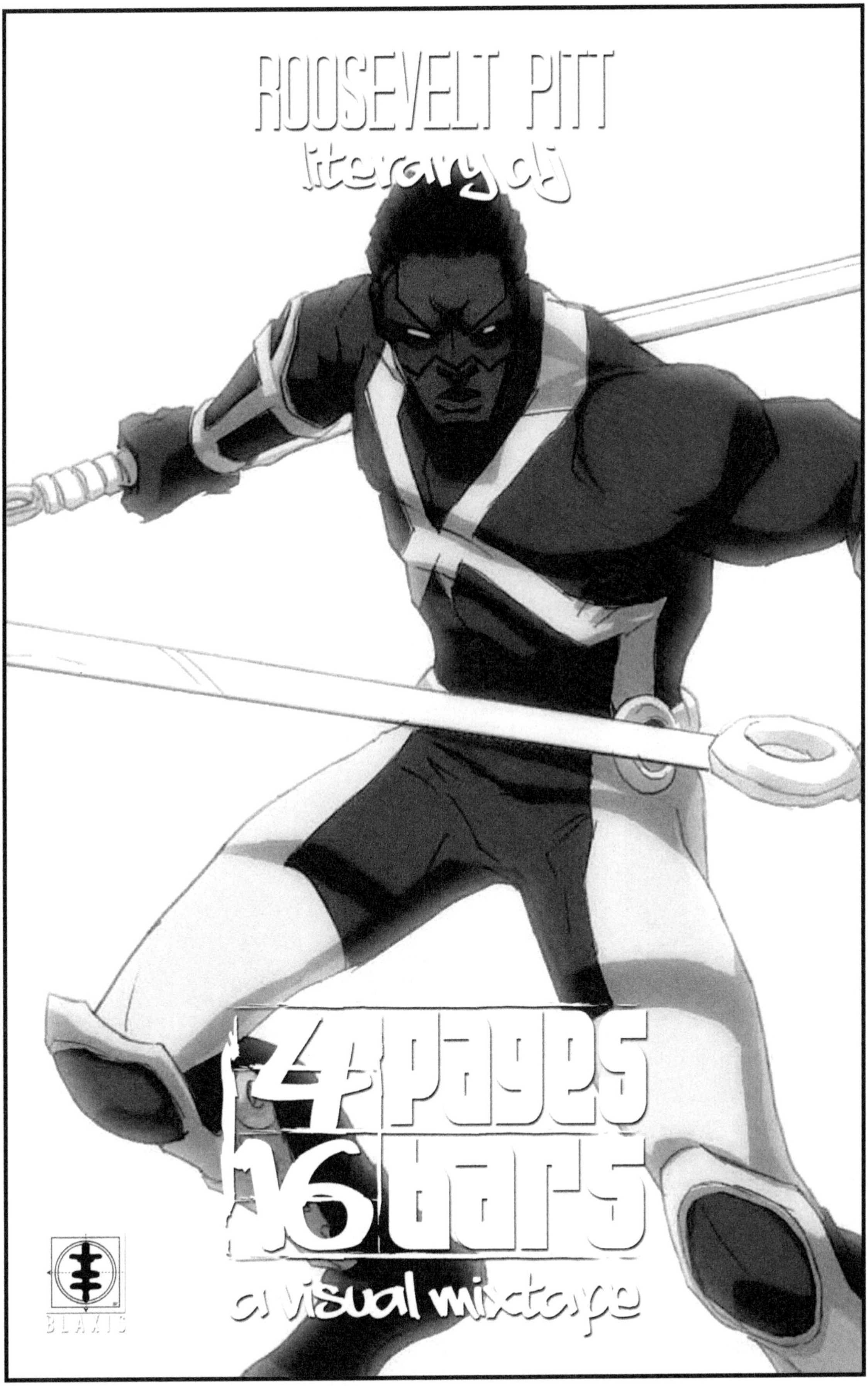
ROOSEVELT PITT
literary dj
4 pages
16 bars
a visual mixtape
BLAXIS

Roosevelt Pitt is the creator of *Purge*.

Purge began its run in July of 1995 with the now defunct
ANIA Comics, a group of African American comic creators
who banded together to publish Afrocentric stories. However,
the creators of Purge jumped ship after their first issue in favor
of self-publishing. Under their new name of **Amara Entertainment**,
Purge began anew.

The series featured the title character, a successful businessman, who felt an
uncontrollable desire to return to his old neighborhood and help where the
police couldn't. As Purge, he could fight crime as he felt it should be fought—
at the criminals' own level. Purge felt that the only lessons that criminals could
learn were violent ones. He used a souped-up motorcycle for transportation
and was an expert in hand-to-hand combat.

Currently, Pitt is working on all-new Purge adventures, to be released in 2015.

website: charlesthechef.net

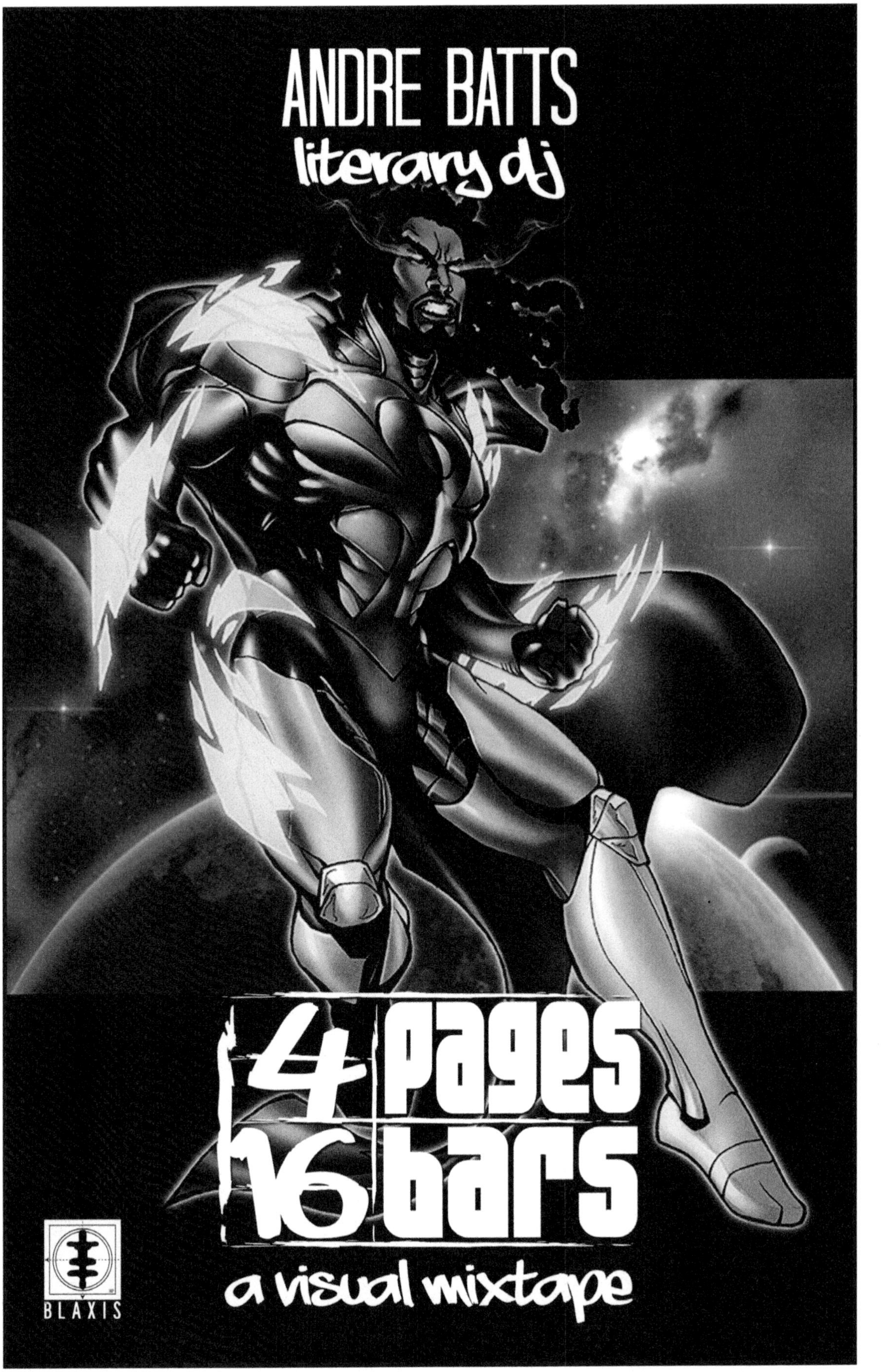
ANDRE BATTS
literary dj
4 pages
16 bars
a visual mixtape
BLAXIS

Andre L.Batts is the creator and founder of **Urban Style Comics**. Although his characters have strong Afro-centric themes that are similar to the current Afro-futurism movement popular in a lot of "underground" comic book creators he feels that anyone who enjoys the genre will enjoy his work.

Urban Style's flagship character, *Dreadlocks*, is guided by the Gods of Alkebulan (Africa) and born as a sacrificial lamb to the Gods of ancient Alkebulan. Dreadlocks has no physical sight for the Gods are his guiding light from within his third eye (spirit/conscious). He is a revolutionary hero based in the urban world. His primary task is bringing Ma'at (universal order, justice and righteousness) to the lost tribes of Alkebulan. Dreadlocks is a hero for the people. He serves only the Gods/ancestors that walked before him.

website: urbanstylecomics.com

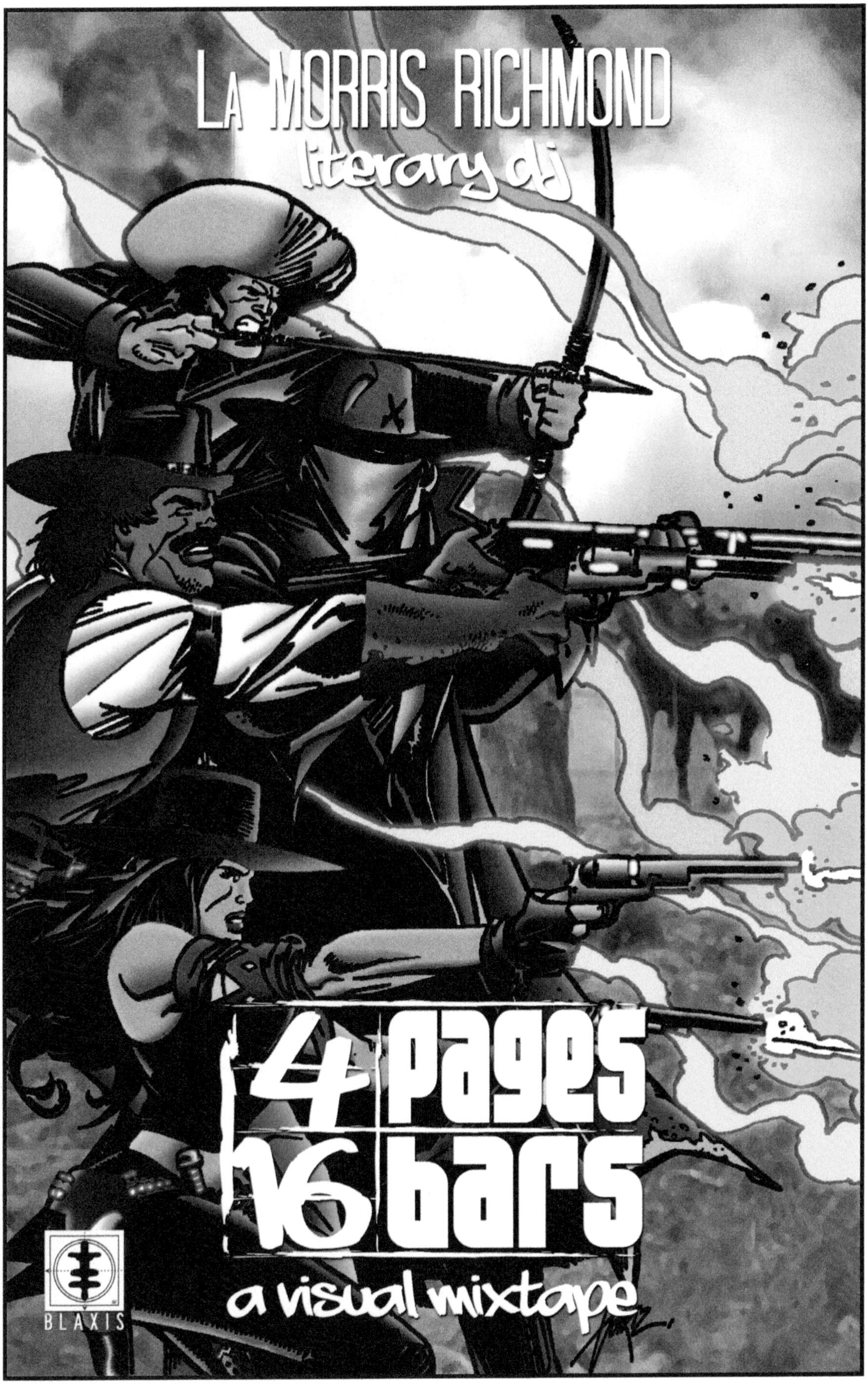
LA MORRIS RICHMOND
literary dj
4 pages
16 bars
a visual mixtape
BLAXIS

La Morris Richmond first broke onto the comics scene with
the *Real Ghostbusters* published by NOW Comics in 1988.
From there he went on to create horror stories for Northstar's *Splatter*,
including *12 Gauge Solution* and the controversial slasher comic book
Boots Of The Oppressor. La Morris spent the next several years working
as City Editor and columnist at The Chicago Defender newspaper before
returning to his first love in life — comics.

After a brief stint as interim Editor-In-Chief of **Griot Enterprises**,
he founded B.L.A.M. Comics! self-publishing the Kung Fu comedy
Canton Kid, and the blood and guts western **Purge: Black, Red & Deadly**.
Excited by his return to Griot Enterprises La Morris shares
the vision of creating a thriving intellectual property company
for the 21st century and beyond.

website: biglamorriscomics.com

TODD JOHNSON
literary dj

4 pages 6 bars

a visual mixtape

BLAXIS

Todd Johnson and Larry Stroman's *Tribe* might have been incredibly short-lived, but its first issue sold more than one million copies in 1993, making it the highest selling comic produced by African American creators in comic book history.

Those who remember that first issue of Tribe understand that Johnson & Stroman were onto something with their story. Over the years a number of petitions have been produced by those trying to resurrect the series.

Despite the book's difficulties to publish, the instant-success of Tribe paved the way for other creators of color to produce their own comics – which is a perfect encapsulation of what made the **Image Revolution** such a game-changer in the 90s.

website: goodreads.com/author/show/7009852.todd-johnson

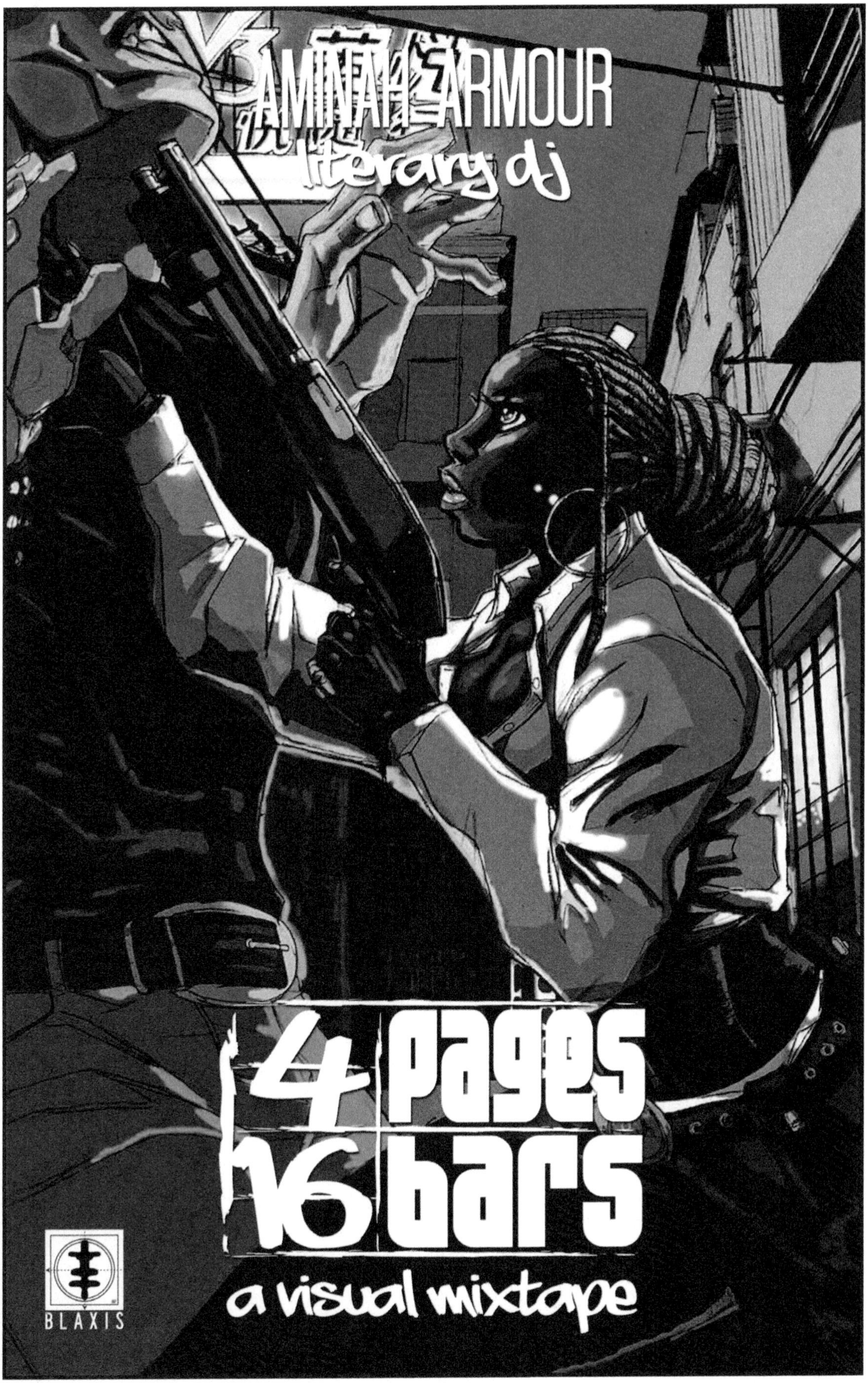
AMINAH ARMOUR
literary dj
4 pages
16 bars
a visual mixtape
BLAXIS

Aminah Armour was born and raised in Chicago. Growing up in the '80s and '90s she was influence by cartoons like Thundercats, He-man and Jem as well as movies and television shows such as Wonder Woman and The Incredible Hulk.. It was only a matter of time before she would gravitate toward comics.

Influenced by writers such as Chris Claremont, Christopher Priest, and Fabian Nicieza, Aminah created **Dziva Jones**, the telepathic/telekenetic, fun, sexy and fierce bodyguard for hire.

website: dzivajones.wix.com/bodyguard

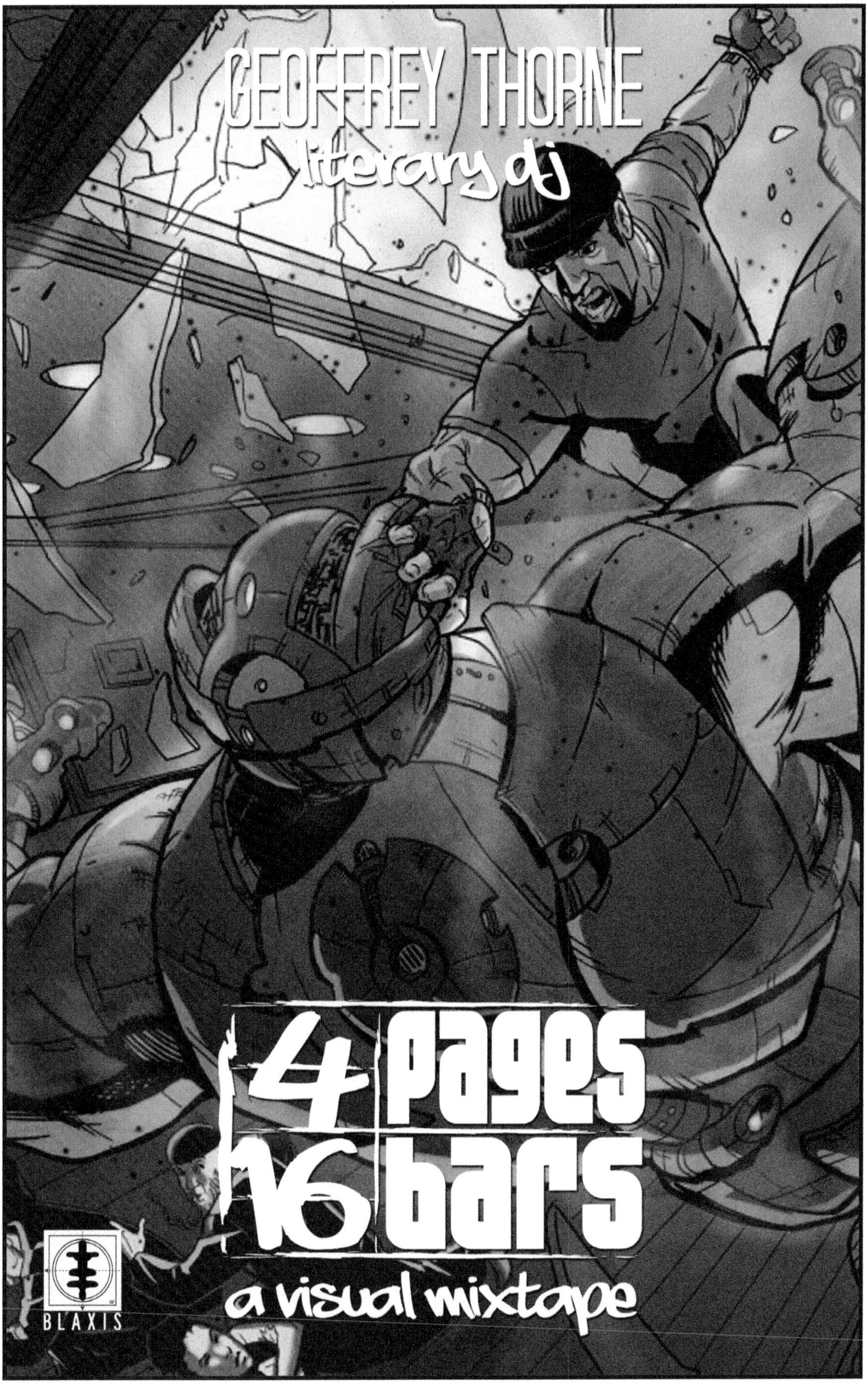
GEOFFREY THORNE
literary dj
4 pages
16 bars
a visual mixtape
BLAXIS

Geoffrey Thorne is a screenwriter, novelist and actor.

After a successful career as a television actor portraying police officer **Wilson Sweet** in the television series In the *Heat of the Night* from 1989 to 1994, Thorne began writing professionally, winning Second Prize in **Simon & Schuster's** sixth annual **Strange New Worlds** anthology with his story *The Soft Room*. He went on to publish more stories in several media tie-in anthologies as well as the **Titan** novel *Star Trek: Sword of Damocles*.

Other stories he has written include contributions to **Flying Pen Press's** anthology *Space Grunts*, MV Media's **Steamfunk** anthology, and **Ellery Queen's Mystery Magazine**.

As a screenwriter, Thorne has worked with **Kickstart Entertainment** to develop two of their properties, *Of Bitter Souls* and *Sword of Dracula*, for television. He was a writer for season 9 of the United States network's *Law & Order*: *Criminal Intent*, season 2 of *Ben 10: Ultimate Alien*, seasons 3,4 and 5 of TNT's *Leverage* as well as the webcomic **Prodigal** for Thrillbent.

In 2014 **Lion Forge Entertainment** and **NBC-Universal** tapped Thorne to reboot the global fan favorite TV series, *KNIGHT RIDER* in comic book form. Thorne is also the co-creator of *Phantom Canyon*, an audio drama from **Pendant Productions**.

Thorne is also a co-founder and writing partner of **GENRE 19**, a studio he formed with artist Todd Harris in 2008.

website: geoffreythorne.com

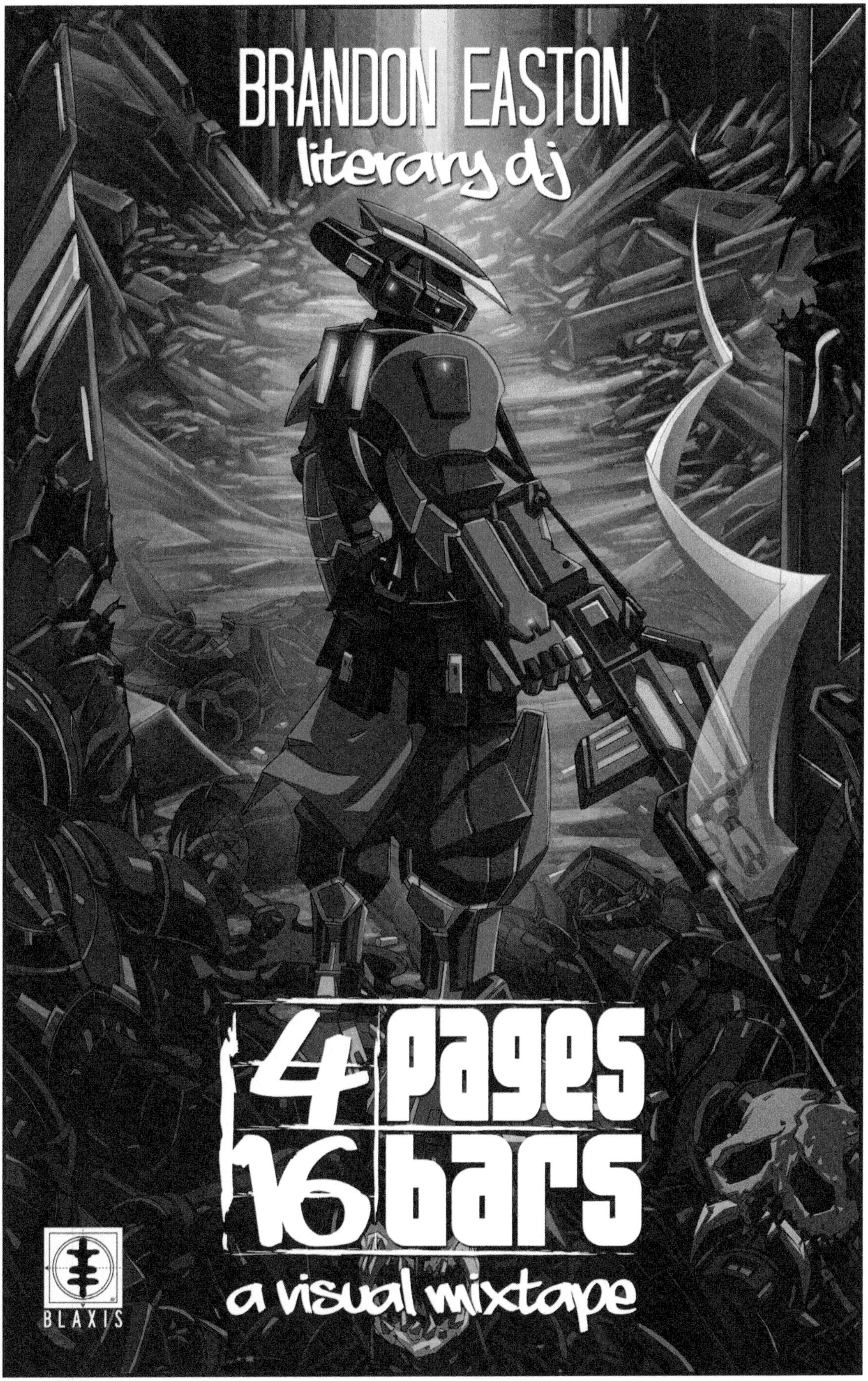
BRANDON EASTON
literary dj
4 pages
16 bars
a visual mixtape
BLAXIS

Brandon M. Easton is a professional writer, screenwriter, and educator based in Los Angeles, CA. After teaching U.S. History and Economics in the Bronx and Harlem, New York for six years, he decided to go for his screenwriting dreams in Hollywood and scored a gig on **Warner Bros.** new *ThunderCats* TV series and Hasbro's new show **Transformers: Rescue Bots.**

His published work includes *Arkanium* and *Transformers: Armada* for **Dreamwave Productions**, **Shadowlaw**, released in January 2012 to an immediate sell-out from **Arcana/Platinum Studios** for which he won the 2012 Glyph Award for Best Writer; *Miles Away*, a teen superhero series from **Antarctic Press**, and multiple titles for **Lion Forge Comics**, including a highly-anticipated *Andre the Giant* graphic novel biography.

Brandon was named the new writer of the international graphic novel franchise *Armarauders* and was a guest writer for **New Paradigm Studios'** *Watson and Holmes* (a reinterpretation of the Holmes mythos set in modern Harlem, NY) comic series for which he received a 2014 Eisner Award nomination for Best Single Issue or One Shot for issue #6. The Eisner Award is considered to be the "Academy Award" of the comic book industry. His work on Watson and Holmes also netted several Glyph Award wins including Story of the Year, Best Writer and the Fan Award.

In 2014, Brandon produced, directed and wrote the documentary ***Brave New Souls: Black Sci-Fi and Fantasy Writers of the 21st Century*** that highlights the inspirations, struggles and creations of a new crop of African-American speculative fiction scribes. Brave New Souls was screened at Eagle Con at Cal State LA, Stan Lee's Comikaze Expo and is slated for multiple festivals and comic cons across the U.S. in the near future. Brandon regularly incorporates his life experience and knowledge of social science into his projects; delivering potent dramatic sequences built from the intersection of race, class and gender.

Brandon was recently announced as one of the eight finalists in the 2015 **Disney/ABC Studios Writing Program** after being chosen from a pool of over 1500 applicants.

website: foolscrusade.blogspot.com

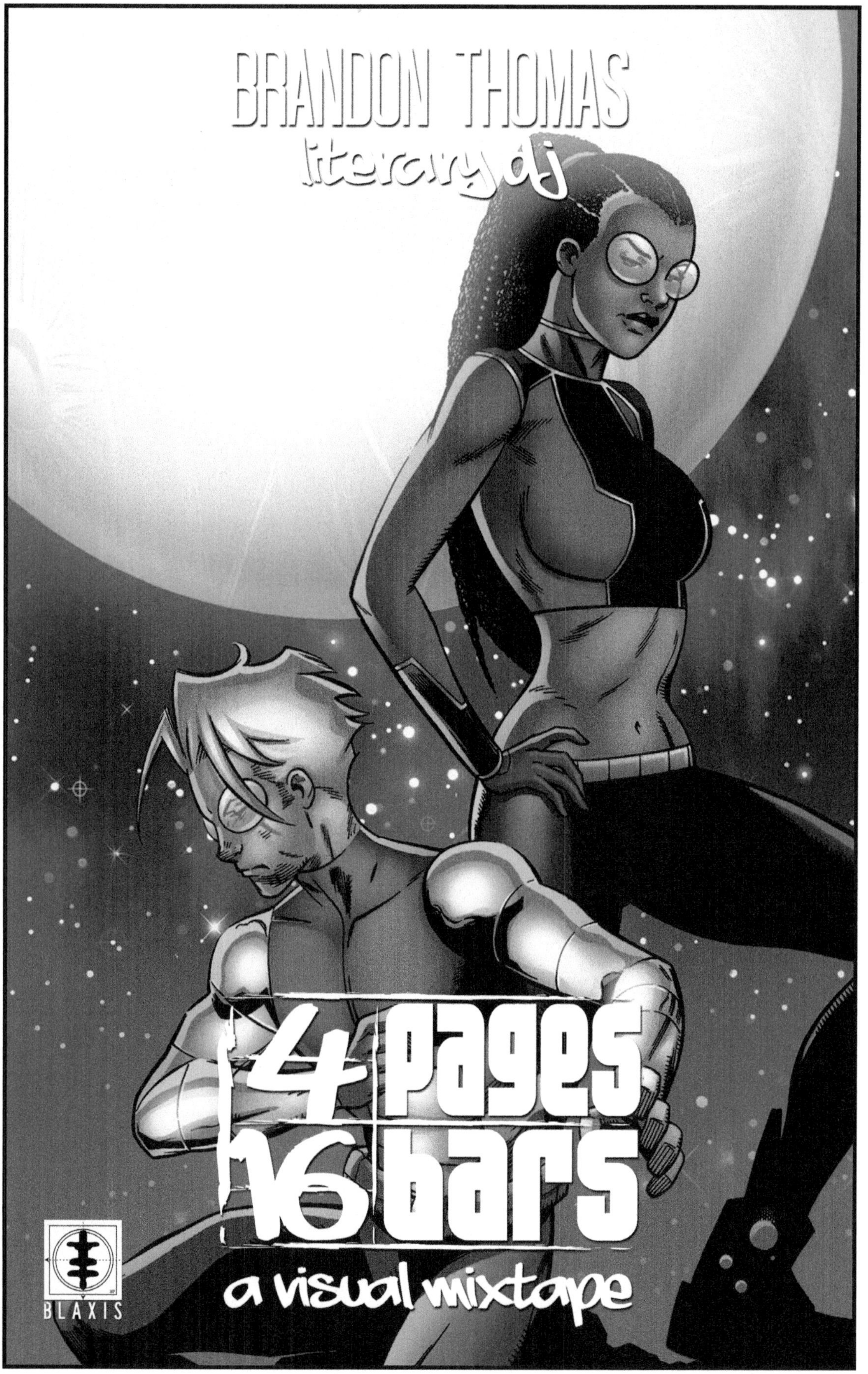
BRANDON THOMAS
literary dj
4 pages
16 bars
a visual mixtape
BLAXIS

Brandon Thomas has written a number of comics for several publishers including **Marvel, Arcade, Dynamite,** and **DC Comics,** and has published over 300 columns. His first creator-owned project **The Many Adventures of Miranda Mercury** returned as an Original Graphic Novel, shipping from **Archaia Entertainment** in August 2011 to widespread critical acclaim. He's currently writing *Voltron* monthly for **Dynamite Entertainment.**

He lives and writes just outside San Diego, CA, with the assistance of his wonderful wife and their puppies Drake and Skye(walker).

website: mirandamercury.com

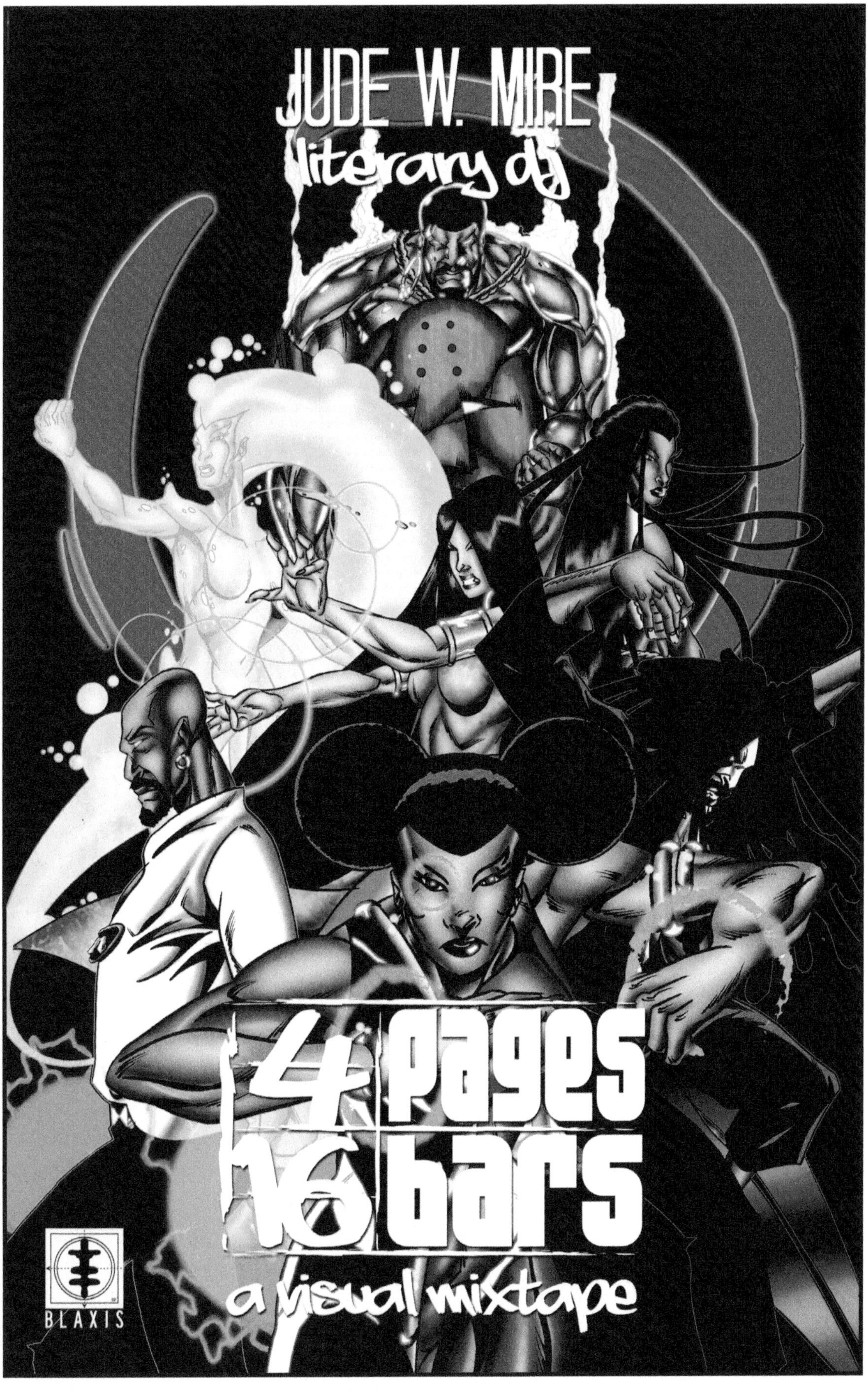
JUDE W. MIRE
literary dj
4 pages
16 bars
a visual mixtape
BLAXIS

Jude W. Mire is an author from Chicago specializing in horror, science fiction, fantasy, and surreal writing. In 2009 and 2010 he was a finalist in the *DeathScribe Horror Radio Play* competition by **WildClaw Theater**. He writes ***The Horsemen: Mark of the Cloven*** for **Griot Enterprises**, has been published in several online magazines, and ran a live horror reading series called **Cult Fiction**.

website: judewire.com

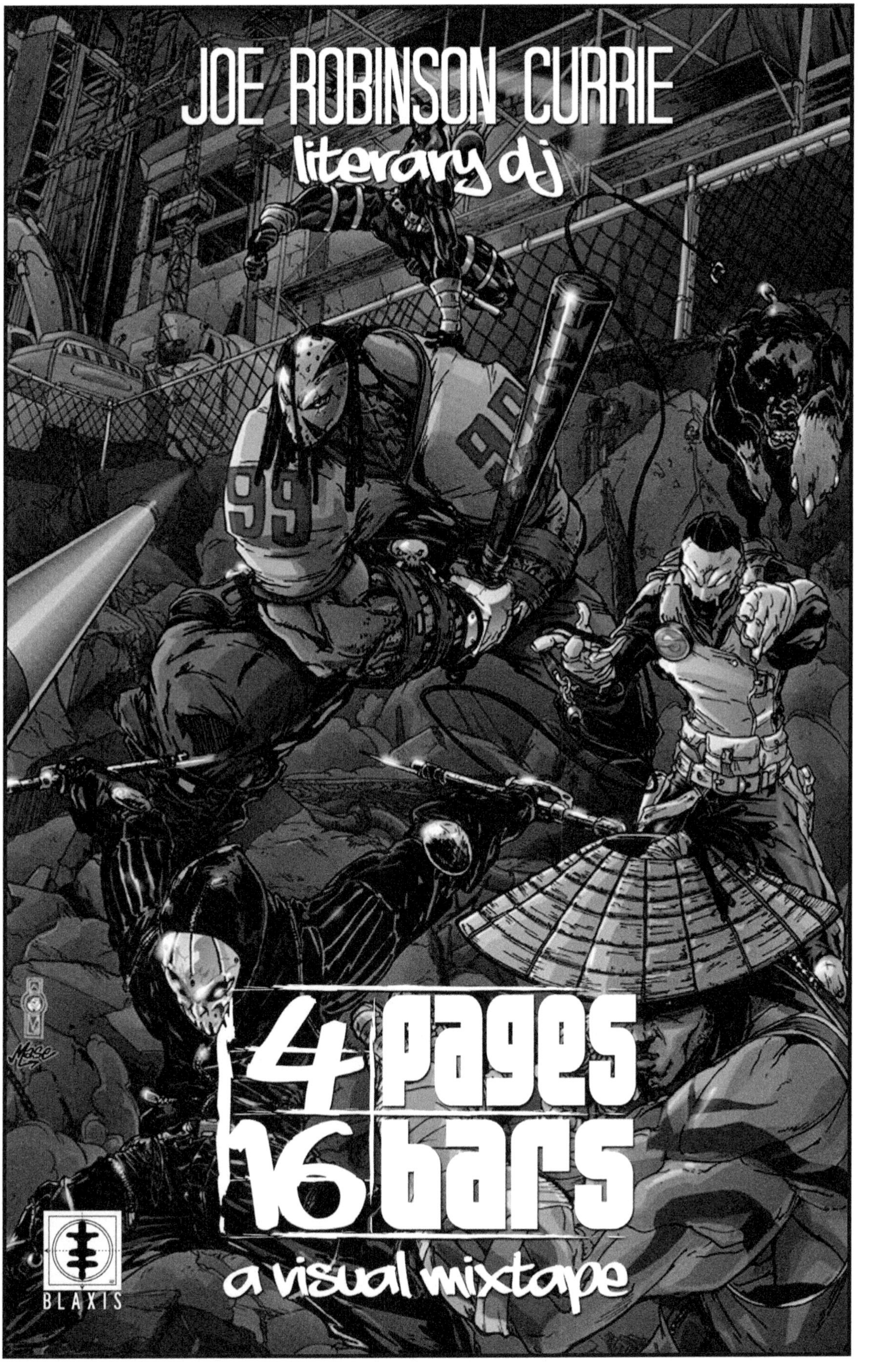
JOE ROBINSON CURRIE
literary dj
99
Mase
4 pages
16 bars
a visual mixtape
BLAXIS

Joe Robinson Currie is comfortable in his chosen field as a comic. After all, Currie started building on his comic career back in 1995, but the proverbial seeds were planted in his mind after years of watching cartoons, reading comics and playing video games.

Joe is the creator of *Punx of Rage* and *Prodigy* for his indie comic book company **Strictly Underground** and a member of *The Almighty Street Team*, a team of vigilantes and urban warriors who come together to face adversaries that are much too powerful to be taken on alone. The concept includes characters created by fellow Visual MCs **Stanley Weaver, James Mason** and **Shawn Alleyne**.

website: punxofrage.net

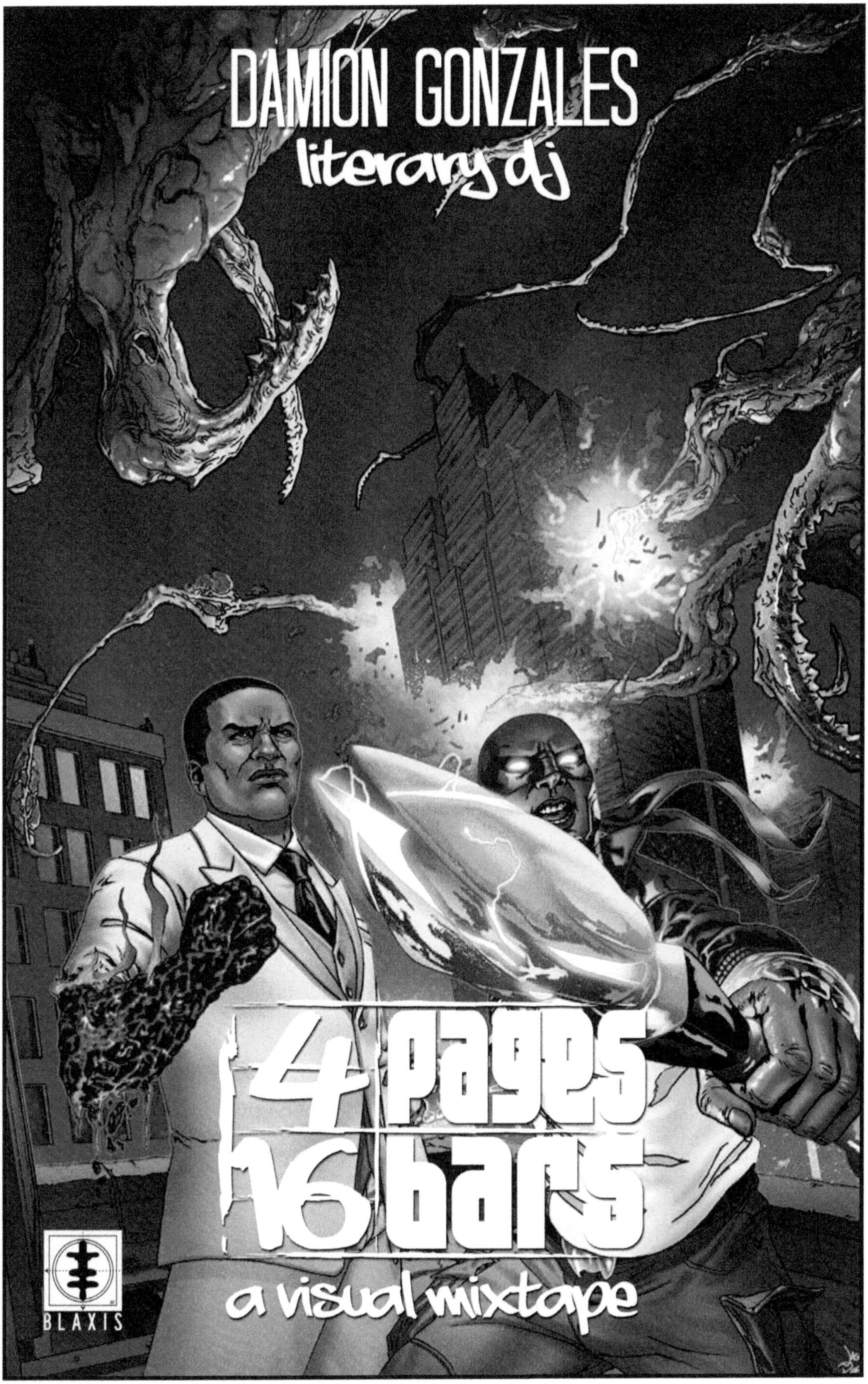
DAMION GONZALES
literary dj
4 pages
16 bars
a visual mixtape
BLAXIS

Damion Gonzales is an occasional actor, award winning theater director, writer and creator from the tiny twin island nation of Trinidad and Tobago.

While growing up in Trinidad he was, at different points in time; a thespian, a director, a rapper, a Hip Hop producer, a dashing rogue and protégé of noted Trinidadian playwright/educator/Pan-Africanist, **Zeno Obi Constance**.

As Constance's protégé, Damion won his first directing award at the age of 18 and would go on to be awarded five more times before he eventually emigrated to the U.S. The first comic he remembers reading is a random issue of Captain Marvel (Mar-Vell) around some point during the late 70's and he's been creating his own characters and stories ever since.

He and his cohorts, who affectionately call themselves **GoliathFox**, have spent the last two years developing the world of **T.A.S.K.** as an animated property. He now lives in Brooklyn, NY with his wife and daughter.

website: operative.net/damiongonzales.html

CPSIA information can be obtained
at www.ICGtesting.com
Printed in the USA
LVOW05s2247180717
541838LV00014B/49/P